ONE
NATION
UNDER
GOD

ONE NATION UNDER GOD

GARY BARVE

Republican Candidate For President Of The United States Of America, Year 2028, As A Supporter Of President Donald J. Trump

LIBERTY HILL PUBLISHING

Liberty Hill Publishing
555 Winderley Pl, Suite 225
Maitland, FL 32751
407.339.4217
www.libertyhillpublishing.com

Due to the changing nature of the Internet, if there are any web addresses, links, or URLs included in this manuscript, these may have been altered and may no longer be accessible. The views and opinions shared in this book belong solely to the author and do not necessarily reflect those of the publisher. The publisher therefore disclaims responsibility for the views or opinions expressed within the work.

Paperback ISBN-13: 979-8-86851-249-0
Ebook ISBN-13: 979-8-86851-250-6

—————————— ◖)•●•(◗ ——————————

My name is Gary Barve. I am a huge supporter of our President Donald J. Trump, a proud Republican of the Republican Party that belongs to our President Donald J. Trump, and I am officially running for President of The United States of America in the 2028 election to help President Donald J. Trump Make America Great Again, Keep America Great and Save America.

And I am running because I love President Donald J. Trump, I love our country the greatest country in the world The United States of America and I love our great American people and I want to help President Donald J. Trump Make America Great Again, Keep America Great and Save America.

This book has five parts or sections.

The first section consists of advice that I have for our great readers of this book based upon my experiences in life and my experiences in the world of American politics as a patriotic member of The Trump Republican Party.

The second section is my life story until today, a life story that sees both struggle and triumph, a life story that has seen complete hopelessness and despair transform into grit, courage, determination and a desire to serve resulting from love for our great United States of America, love for President Donald J. Trump and love for our great American people.

The third section consists of my thoughts about many America First Agenda issues.

The fourth section consists of my thoughts about President Donald J. Trump.

The fifth section consists of some posts that I have made on my campaign social media that I feel you will find interesting, informative and perhaps even somewhat controversial.

I am dedicating this book to My Lord And Savior Jesus Christ, to President Donald J. Trump for inspiring me to go for my dreams, my parents Mohini and Harsh Barve for supporting me especially during my battle with my previous clinical depression related illness, to my friends, to the many team members working with me currently and to the many team members who have worked with me previously, to our great American people that built our great country, and to my and our country the greatest country in the world The United States of America.

Gary Barve's Social Media is:

Campaign Website: www.GaryBarveForAmerica.com

Campaign Truth Social Page:

https://truthsocial.com/@GaryBarve

Campaign Facebook Page:

https://www.facebook.com/GaryBarveForUSA

Campaign X.com

Page: https://x.com/garybarveusa?s=21

SECTION ONE

ONE

◇◇◇

Believe in yourself. If you do not believe in yourself, there will be very few people in the world (if any) who will believe in you.

Believe you will make it happen in life, believe you will make your dreams and the dreams of the people around you come true.

And as President Trump says, Dream Big And Bold, for yourself, and if possible for our country.

And then, once you have your positive and productive dream ready in your mind and in your imagination, make it happen or be ready to die trying.

If your dreams are big and bold, this is the only mentality in my opinion that will give you a tremendous chance of making your dreams come to reality and fruition in real life.

I will give you an example:

In the previous few years fighting for my and our great United States of America and for President Trump's America First agenda, I have through my political campaigns fought against criminals, gangs, cartels such as

MS-13 and Tren De Aragua, drug dealers, drug smugglers and human traffickers. I have not held back from saying things very strongly against these horrific groups.

I say this to myself: If I want to serve my country as President of The United States of America and as Commander In Chief, I should be ready to take a bullet for my country, or maybe even worse, who knows. I am prepared to do this, because one of my dreams is to be President of The United States of America to Make America Great Again, Keep America Great and Save America as a Republican supporter of our President Donald J. Trump.

I will conclude my example by saying this: I have zero doubt in my mind that someday, perhaps in 2028, if not then at a slightly later time, I will succeed in achieving my above mentioned dream. I have zero doubt about it in my mind.

So, my advice is this: Be prepared to give up your life for what you believe in – that is the level of commitment that will give you your best chance of being successful especially if you want to achieve your big positive and productive dreams in your life.

And again, as President Trump says. Dream Big And Bold!

TWO

I believe that you should never be afraid of losing what you have in life, because it is when you start fearing losing what you have in life, that you actually begin losing what you have in life.

People work really hard to achieve things in life. It is natural, especially when you achieve a certain level of success in life, that you want to hold on to it and try your best not to lose it. This attitude is a big mistake. What separates the big winners from the losers is how you react to the situation where you have achieved some level of success.

My advice is keep taking calculated or sometimes relatively reckless risks irrespective of the level of success you have in your life. However, keep in mind that when you take the risks – calculated or relatively reckless – that you are 100% committed to achieving what you are looking to achieve. No half measures because if you are not completely committed, the risks are almost always not going to pay off.

On the other hand, if you are brave and courageous and 100% committed towards what you are trying to achieve, you have a very good chance of being successful.

Here's why:

First, if you are taking a big risk, remember that it is a big risk because there are very few people willing to take that risk, that's one of the reasons the risk is big. If everyone was taking the risk, it would not be a risk, would it? So you are competing with fewer people than you would imagine. You have already differentiated your-self from most other people.

Second, of the relatively small number of people who are taking the big risks in life, an ever smaller number of them are 100% committed to achieving the goal or objective. So if you are taking big risks, and at the same time you are 100% committed to achieving your goal and objective, you actually have a tremendous shot at being extremely successful.

Still doubt whether what I am saying has truth to it?

Think about it – Are there not certain people in our country and the world who make success into a habit? They succeed again and again, and then yet again. President Donald J. Trump is the most successful man on earth. Look at his successes, one after the other: He built one of the most successful real estate businesses, he wrote many best selling books, he had the Number 1 hit TV show The Apprentice, he became the 45th President of The United States of America, and has now made one of the greatest comebacks in the history of our country by becoming the 47th President of The United States of America. He also had a Number 1 song, Justice For All!

My advice is: Keep taking risks, calculated and sometimes relatively reckless risks, and stay 100% committed to achieving your goal and objective. You will almost definitely be successful.

THREE

◇◇

Never Give Up!

This is President Trump's Number 1 advice to our American people. And I have the same advice for you. Keep pushing forward, irrespective of how difficult it might seem to get. If you give up, you are not 100% committed per ONE, and you will almost definitely lose, or at the very least, not achieve your true potential. Not achieving one's true potential is a travesty, especially in a country like our great country, The United States of America.

FOUR

<><><><><><><><><><><><><><><><><><><><><><><><><><><><><><><><><><><><><><>

You must love what you do in your career and in your life. This is President Trump's Number 2 advice. I learnt about this from a video interview of his on the internet, and I thought about it.

Here's why I feel it is very important to love what you do in your career and in your life:

You have a limited time to spend on earth, from the moment you are born to the moment you die. If you spend this limited time doing what you love in your life, does that not give you a great chance to stay happy in life? It is almost impossible to be extremely unhappy in life while you are doing what you love in your life!

Same with your career, find work in life that you love doing and you will stay quite happy.

My advice is, if possible try and monetize what you love doing in your career if you do not have the financial resources. It should be possible to do so in most circumstances. Your initial reaction could be, for example – I like to fish and hunt and don't see a way to monetize it. I disagree. If you are really passionate about it and want to make it happen, you will innovatively differentiate yourself from the people who would like to fish and hunt for a living, and reach that place where monetizing your passion is possible. None of this is easy, of course, else everyone would do it. But I believe it is possible.

Of course, if you are running for President of The United States of America like I am, you cannot really make much money from employment because it is a full time responsibility. But in general, I feel you could make it happen for yourself.

Also remember this – when you are trying to achieve a goal or objective, perhaps a big goal or objective, there will be moments in time, perhaps a few quick moments, when you feel like quitting. This moment is the most pivotal moment of your journey towards achieving your goal or objective – DO NOT REACT TO THIS EMOTION OF WANTING TO QUIT! Let the moment pass.

For this, you need to identify the emotion as it hits you. It will start as a thought, then build into an emotion. Identify it, let is pass, do not quit! Tomorrow will almost always be a better day – keep moving forward!

My advice: Don't get into a dull routine that zaps the passion and zeal out of your life. Find what you love to do, and go for it with 100% commitment. It will transform your life in ways you wouldn't believe!

FIVE

◇◇

This is a very important topic, especially in the world of politics, but in any walk of life: TRUST.

Here's what I believe:

Only one person in the world wants what you want for you in your life: And that one person in YOU. Why would anyone else care, unless there is their self interest associated with it? It is a hard concept to accept, but it is the truth and so I am writing about it in my book.

My thought: Do not trust anyone completely unless there is the other persons self interest associated with the task you are trying to achieve, in which case you could trust him or her for that particular event with some level of confidence. If the event or task is more important than some of the other events or tasks you could be involved with with that person, you might find it easier to translate that trust into the other tasks too, because the original task is important enough that they will not want to lose you by betraying you on a lesser important task.

Remember this: They almost definitely will not stab you in the back if they are going to get stabbed in the back along with you. This is especially true in the world of politics, because the world of politics is a cut throat world.

Now, also remember this—Be the bigger person whenever possible and treat everyone with respect to the best of your ability. Respect is very important, try not to disrespect someone unless it is really warranted. In the world of politics, it is certainly sometimes warranted, especially during media interviews and debates.

SIX

Eye for an eye! Get back at people whenever possible. President Donald J. Trump believes in this too.

There are multiple reasons for doing this.

First, if someone purposefully (not by a genuine mistake, but on purpose) does you wrong, I believe it is your responsibility to fight back and get even. More true if it is personal and not business.

Second, if you don't get back at people for doing you wrong, the people watching will feel you are a loser who will not have the courage to fight back if someone does you wrong. If an opportunity presents itself, some of these people will do you wrong too, especially if they are not your friends, and some, even if they are your friends. Get back, as President Trump says, 10 to 15 times harder!

The world is watching, and when they see that you fight back and get even, or at least make a sincere attempt to fight back and get even, they will be less likely to go against you for the fun of it, and perhaps even if its for business reasons.

In fact, many of your friends, and to be honest, many of your enemies will begin to respect you for this attitude, and you can keep many of your friends and maybe even convert some of your enemies into your friends.

14

SEVEN

Remember this word: LOYALTY.

A loyal friend is extremely hard to find, especially in the world of politics. Value the quality of loyalty, especially when demonstrated over time and under fire.

Treat such loyal friends with the utmost respect – when the world turns on you, and it will at some point in time – these are the people who will fight with you.

Do not make the mistake of completely trusting a person being friendly with you because you are in a position of power and authority or because you are in a position to give them something they want. They will desert you, or even try and destroy you at first, if not the first, certainly the second opportunity.

You do not need to be disrespectful to such people, treat them with respect too. But make a mental note of the situation and the friendship dynamic.

President Trump values Loyalty as the single most important attribute a friend could have. I believe in this also.

EIGHT

Keep your promises. It will allow people to support you more easily if you have a track record of being a man or a woman who keeps his or her promises.

Keeping promises is a rare quality. Make it your strength. Go out of your way to keep promises, especially if it 'feels' right from instinct perspective.

Also, think very carefully before making a promise. A promise someone pulls out of you in the spur of the moment is not really a promise, so think carefully and then make the promise. Think about the positives and the negatives, think from all possible angles. And then make the decision about whether you want to make the promise.

My advice: Once you make the promise, Keep The Promise.

Expect the same from others, but do not get disappointed if people let you down and don't keep their promise.

I will say this – if someone makes a habit out of not keeping promises, that is betrayal – Get back at them whenever the opportunity presents itself.

Most people will let you down, that's my experience, especially if you are not careful about who you associate with. Try and associate with good people, use your data and then gut instinct to make the decision of who you would like to associate with.

NINE

I believe that sometimes in life, especially when you have big goals, you have to walk your path alone for some time. Not everyone will want to come along with you on your journey in life, especially in the early stages of your walk towards your dream, goals and aspirations.

My advice is: Do not get discouraged by this. Keep moving forward, and on almost all circumstances, do not hold any grudge against the people who decided not to initially walk with you on your journey.

You will find that as you become successful, these people will want to join you in your journey, and perhaps that's a good thing. As President Trump says, Success will bring people together.

TEN

Go for your dreams. If you fail in the process of achieving your dream, that is acceptable. If you hesitate to go for your dreams, and achieve what in your mind is mediocrity, I feel that is failure anyways.

Not everyone's dream is to run for President of The United States of America or to become President of The United States of America. A dream can be as simple as – I want to live a happy and content life. Or, I want to be a Farmer or a Coal Mine Worker or a Oil and Gas worker or serve our country in Law Enforcement, the American Military or become a Doctor or a Nurse or a Fire Fighter for example.

What I am saying is, if you have that dream, and if you do not take the effort and actual action towards achieving your dream, you are doing yourself a tremendous disservice.

The key word here is take ACTION – do something about it in the form of definite action oriented steps towards achieving your dream.

Thinking about your dreams and aspirations is incredible too, as President Trump says, dreams are free: You should dream about your dreams and aspirations in life and actually see yourself being successful at it in your mind.

But then, start taking action towards achieving your dreams.

This is what separates the people who reach their dreams and aspirations, and the people who do not.

ELEVEN

Try not to get influenced by unknown entities or unknown people, this will only distract you. For example, in the world of politics, or in the world of working for firms and companies and organizations, there will be people around you who you cannot always pick and choose (unless you are an entrepreneur or a political candidate, in which case it is possible to a larger extent) and you certainly cannot control how they will behave or react to situations and circumstances even if you do get to pick or choose them.

Some of these people will be positive and friendly, hopefully most would be, if you are working for the right firm or organization (if not, think about exiting and finding another firm or organization after a sufficient sample space of time has passed – you are too precious to suffer for too long) but some would be negative and will try and pull you down relentlessly. And it is not always possible to avoid such negative people.

This is always a difficult situation to deal with but my advice is: Try not to give the negative nay sayers your mindspace. If you let these negative people – what they say to you, how they behave with you, and so on and so forth – get into your mindspace, it will negatively impact you in a much bigger way than if you learn to ignore them.

I understand what you are thinking – this is easier said than done. Yes, I get that. But if you think positively about this, and try and implement it in your work life, it could make a somewhat positive difference in your life.

TWELVE

<<<<<<<<<<<<<<<<<<<<<<<<<<<<<<<<<<<<<<<<<<<>>

(Almost) always remain humble and respectful, but if someone tries to pull you down, make sure you know exactly who you are and allow that realization and knowledge to keep your mental self confidence and mental equilibrium.

Try and identify your emotions—how you feel—when someone tries to bring you down a notch or two. Think about it – you are feeling great about your life, you have a conversation with a negative person, and a few moments later you feel very unhappy.

What happened here?

You reacted to words being said to you by this negative person, and felt unhappy. This continued for a few minutes of conversation, and you feel even more unhappy, perhaps sad or dejected even.

Here's my advice, and I have learnt this from experience:

Try and identify the very first moment when a negative person says something to you that pulls you down.

Remember this – it is not necessarily the negative persons words that are pulling you down, it is your reaction to those negative words by the negative person that makes you feel unhappy.

Identify this AS IT HAPPENS, and consciously realize that it is happening, and then at the same time use your self confidence – bring it to your conscious mind, and you will soon see that you take the negative words with a smile on your face and it does not affect you anywhere near the way it used to affect you. I call it staying mentally equanimous under most circumstances.

THIRTEEN

Think for yourself before asking people for advice. There is a good chance that you will find the right answer yourself.

Now, this does not mean you should not ask people for advice as long as you are convinced you can trust the person you are asking for advice to give you his or her real honest thought, advice and opinion about the situation at hand.

But if you have thought about it and come up with one or two solutions before asking for advice, not only will your conversation with the person you are seeking advice from be more productive, but you will soon start relying less on other peoples advice, especially about a subject or a topic that you are well versed with.

FOURTEEN

◇◇

How to handle pressure: I learnt about how to handle pressure from President Donald J. Trump. I feel that he believes that when you are under pressure in life, try and think about it in the terms that: It doesn't really matter, nothing really matters in life other than the really big things such as faith and family and country.

I find this advice to be incredible because when you think in this way it sort of detaches your mind from the pressure that you could be feeling.

Here is another additional way of handling pressure that I realized a few years back and find to be helpful:

Many times in life, you will find that you are feeling mental pressure. In such situations, whenever possible, try and arrive at a mindset where you are 100% convinced in your thought process and 100% convinced about the decision you are going to make about the issue that is giving you the mental pressure.

Make a decision based upon the decision making process mentioned later on in this book and arrive at a definite conclusion and resolution that you are 100% convinced about.

I have found from experience that many times, you wallow in your fears and the mental pressure without actually doing anything about it. You go about in circles in your mind, and each such circular thought adds to the pressure, becoming a vicious cycle.

Snap out of it as soon as you identify that this is happening, and then begin focusing on a resolution or a solution to the issue or situation at hand. Once you get to thinking this way, try not to rest or relax until you come to a solution you are 100% convinced about.

You will realize that when this happens, there is little to no pressure remaining in your mind.

It is all in the mind, and it is all about how well you understand your mind.

FIFTEEN

This is a President Donald J. Trump belief and I believe it too, he says that part of being a winner is knowing when enough is enough and its time to quit. Now, this previous sentence is very much against most of what I have written in this book, so I am going to elaborate on it, because it certainly makes sense when taken in the right context.

Lets say you are the owner of a business. You have run the business for 10 years and have seen losses after losses with no potential for a future success. You are feeling like it is not your passion in life anymore and that you do not love what you do anymore.

I feel that if you are convinced you no longer love what you do in your career, it could be time to quit and try something different in your career. Life is too short to spend a sustained and long amount of time doing things that make you sad or miserable.

Hopefully the above paragraph puts things in the correct context. You should Never Give Up, remember that, it is the key rule and principle. But if you stop loving what you are doing in your career, it is okay to adjust plans and renavigate a little.

SIXTEEN

Do not run away from having tough conversations. Now, there is a time and a place for the tough conversation, pick and choose the where and the when if possible, but if you procrastinate from having the tough conversation, you will start feeling miserable. Don't do that. Take control and charge of the situation to the best of your ability given your circumstance, and have the tough conversation. You will almost always feel better after you have the tough conversation.

SEVENTEEN

Do not make the mistake of playing with the mentality: "I want to be nice to this person because I want him or her to be my friend if I lose in my life." No! Play to win. Behave as a winner. Do not be arrogant, be respectful. But do not go on the back foot or take wrong behavior from people thinking – "It's ok, I want his or her help if I lose in my life".

Here's what I believe: If you are a big loser in life, 99% of the people you know including your wife or girlfriend, relatives, friends will run away from you. The only difference is that some will run away from you faster than some others. Think positive and play the winner card. You will have your best shot at winning.

EIGHTEEN

Set the bar high for yourself, and expect the best from yourself. Expect the best from your team too but in your mind do not set the bar equally high for your team.

I am beginning to believe that in the political realm, the candidate running for office should be the most hardest working member of the team, and he or she should be the most passionate and initiative taking member of the team driven to take him or her and his or her team to a win.

I currently work with a great team for my campaign for President of The United States of America. They are incredible talented people who love America and President Trump, and hopefully me!

If I set the bar too high for my team, a few things happen:

First, I am setting myself up for potential disappointment.

Second, if I don't allow the occasional mistake or error from the team member, I will be unable to make an occasional mistake or error myself. I believe President Trump believes in this second point too.

This said, if the team member shows a pattern of making mistakes or errors that are not necessarily genuine or fixable, take the risk of firing or letting go the individual from the team. This should be your last resort, but sometimes it is necessary.

I work almost all the time on my campaign. I certainly take some time away from serving my country (I try not to call my campaigning 'work', I enjoy it too much to call it that) from time to time, but I have observed that even when I am not actively working on the campaign, my thoughts are with the campaign and with how I could help President Trump Make America Great Again, Keep America Great and Save America. I have received some of my biggest inspirations while I have been not actively working on the campaign.

NINETEEN

Have a tremendous positive attitude ideally at all times, if not then at most times.

This becomes extremely difficult to achieve in the face of adversity, such as for example the clinical depression related illness that I was diagnosed with in approximately the year 2012. I struggled and battled with this illness for many years, and I have seen some horrific times in my life. I am happy to say that I have now made a complete recovery from my clinical depression related illness and take no treatment now.

I thank my Lord and Savior Jesus Christ (I respect all religions but I am Christian), my parents, my friends and the medical staff for giving me the ability to conquer this illness. I also thank President Trump for his inspiring interviews, videos, speeches and his book Think Big which I believe is the greatest book ever written after The Bible.

I have begun to realize that having a positive attitude allows you to conquer some of the toughest challenges that you will undoubtedly face in your life.

TWENTY

Here's a thought I use sometimes for me: Whenever you get too emotional about something, find your steel. Get tougher. Just saying this to yourself will make you tougher in the moment.

TWENTY ONE

Do not overthink things, do not dwell on a thought for too long. Give it adequate consideration, learn what you can from it, and then move forward with your day. Overthinking can clutter your mind and complicate things more than how complicated they actually are.

TWENTY TWO

Make every move or decision carefully but with a lot of confidence. Determined and purposeful moves are admired and respected. People could dislike you or even hate you for your decision, but they will unwillingly admire your decisiveness. That's the word you should remember from this paragraph: DECISIVENESS. Think before committing to one path. Maybe take a few days to think depending on the situation. And then once you make the decision, try and be as decisive about it as possible.

TWENTY THREE

How to make Decisions: This is what President Trump says about making decisions—Analyze the situation you are in with as much data as possible and get as much knowledge about the situation as possible, but in a certain limited amount of time. And when you have balanced the level of acquired knowledge with the appropriate amount of time it takes to acquire this knowledge, use your GUT INSTINCT to make your decision. I believe in this way of making decisions 100%.

TWENTY FOUR

Do not have too many expectations from any meeting or from any situation. Having low or even no expectation from a meeting or situation will reduce your chance of disappointment and it could also free you up mentally to put your best self forward in the meeting or the situation.

TWENTY FIVE

39

Be as self reliant as possible. The more self reliant you are, the less you depend on other people for your happiness and joy.

TWENTY SIX

I don't like politics. I really don't. I tolerate politics because I love serving our great United States of America, and I love serving President Donald J. Trump's America First Agenda to Make America Great Again, Keep America Great and Save America. Politics is my conduit for serving our American people.

TWENTY SEVEN

Do not forget to have fun in life. Life should not be all about your career or the political campaign. Feel free to take some time off to follow your hobbies and passions in life. As President Trump says, you should have wholeness in life.

TWENTY EIGHT

Life is tough. Try and think about the blessings in your life whenever possible, it will make you feel better than how you were feeling before you started thinking about the blessings in your life.

TWENTY NINE

Whenever you walk out of the door in the morning, whether it is for work on a weekday, or it is for work on a weekend, or it is to meet your friends or family, make sure you are focused, alert and ready to take on the day.

THIRTY

Try and prepare for all meetings in advance.

THIRTY ONE

Try and be in control of your emotions.

You will find that in life, and in politics, there will be some people who will try and put pressure on you, perhaps try and intimidate you, and try and upset or even infuriate you.

I have found that on most occasions, you will be able to handle these situations well if you keep your emotions in control and if you keep emotionally calm and composed while the interaction with the difficult person is happening.

THIRTY TWO

Sometimes people will hold back their appreciation or validation to see if you will go an additional mile.

Some people do this to get the best out of you. Some people do this to get the best for themselves.

Try and identify when this occurs, and then think very carefully before you decide to go that additional mile.

I am a big believer in taking calculated risks and sometimes what I call reckless risks. But do remember that in the context of this paragraph, going the additional mile will usually involve taking more risk, and perhaps you will realize that you do not need to take that risk to reach your goal.

THIRTY THREE

◇◇◇

I am currently 40 years of age. At this stage of my life, I have identified and believe in the following few points as the path towards achieving success and the path towards perhaps being the most successful person on earth.

1. Find work in life you love doing and dedicate yourself to this work
2. Never Give Up: Once you find this work in life you love doing, then dedicate yourself to it, commit yourself to it and never give up. Be 100% committed towards your goals
3. Be ready to take calculated risks and at times reckless risks as mentioned previously in the book. When done correctly and wisely, this will differentiate yourself from many others and catapult you towards success in the long run
4. The first 3 points in THIRTY THREE will probably make you very successful in your career. You have a great shot at living a very nice life, especially in a country like our country, The United States of America. This 4th point in THIRTY THREE will make you one of the most successful people on earth, if not the most successful person on earth.

Be ready to die for what you are trying to achieve, or I will rephrase and say be ready for worse than dying for what you are trying to achieve.

I will give you an example: I believe with 100% confidence that I will someday become The President of The United States of America and Save America. I have ZERO DOUBT about this in my mind. And I want to be President not for some power grab, but so that someday I will be able to Save America, my country that I love. And I am 100% ready to die for this cause or goal, or like I said, face worse than death.

I have already proven this during my campaign for President of The United States of America as a Republican supporter of President Donald J. Trump. I have taken on criminals, gangs, cartels such as MS-13 and Tren De Aragua, drug dealers, drug smugglers and human traffickers in a way that I believe NOBODY in America perhaps other than President Donald J. Trump has done before.

I have said on air, radio, podcasts, social media, public speeches:

I AM DIRECTLY TALKING TO GANG MEMBERS OF GANGS SUCH AS MS-13 AND TREN DE ARAGUA THAT ARE LISTENING IN RIGHT NOW. MY DIRECT MESSAGE TO YOU IS:

GET THE HELL OUT OF OUR UNITED STATES OF AMERICA. IF YOU DON'T, WE WILL INCARCERATE MEMBERS OF

YOUR GANGS OR WE WILL KICK OUT OF OUR COUNTRY MEMBERS OF YOUR GANGS.

I have no Secret Service protection at the time of writing this book, I have no money to hire private security for me, and I am certain these gang members that are in our country illegally do NOT like me, and that is an understatement.

I just believe that my Lord And Savior Jesus Christ will protect me, and allow me the ability to serve my United States of America and keep YOU our great American people safe and secure, even if that means that I will take a bullet for you, or worse.

FINAL WORD FROM GARY BARVE FOR SECTION 1:

◇◇

I am running for President of The United States of America in the 2028 election as a Republican supporter of President Donald J. Trump. I wrote this (some words changed for the book) around the time I made the decision to run for President of The United States of America:

Gary, if you become President of The United States of America by winning the election in 2028, as President, always make the final decision for your country yourself. You can take advice from advisors, supporters, consultants, team members, well wishers and friends: but always make the final decision for your country yourself by following President Trump's decision making mechanism explained earlier on in this book: analyze the data in an appropriate amount of time and then make a gut instinct decision.

Remember this Gary: The American people who voted for you to lead the country as President did so because they believe in you and because they want you to continue President Trump's legacy by always keeping America First and keeping our American People First. They want you to

Make America Great Again, Keep America Great and Save America. Make the decisions for your country yourself and on almost all occasions take ownership and responsibility for the decisions.

I will complete this first section of the book with a line I have utilized to complete many of my speeches over the previous few months and years:

We Are One Nation Under God, And In God We Trust.

May God Bless You, And May God Bless The United States of America, The Greatest Country On Earth.

Thank You, And Lets Win This!

SECTION 2

My name is Gary Barve, and I am running for President of The United States of America in the 2028 election as a Republican supporter of President Donald J. Trump.

I was born in Summit, New Jersey in 1984. My parents, Mohini and Harsha Barve, immigrated to The United States of America from India in I think about 1982.

Per my memory, we lived in a relatively small 2 bedroom rental apartment in New Jersey.

I started kindergarten in New Jersey and went to a school named Start Right in New Jersey for a little while.

I would have loved to grow up in our great United States of America, but my family relocated to India when I was about four and a half years old. I completed most of my education in India.

On some of the radio shows and podcasts that I have had the great honor of being a guest on, the host of the show has asked me questions about my time in India. I have attended numerous Republican events in different areas of our great United States of America over the course of the previous few years, and many great American people have asked me questions about my time growing up in India.

I have always consistently answered these questions by saying:

I was born in Summit, New Jersey in 1984, and I have President Donald J. Trump Republican American blood in me. I did grow up in India, and lived there for a few years, but I do not talk about my time in India too much at all because it detracts from the love that I have for my country and your country and our country, The United States of America.

Depending on the situation and circumstances, I might have to talk about some details about my time in India during my campaign for President of The United States of America in the 2028 election as a Republican supporter of President Donald J. Trump, but lets cross that bridge when the time comes.

As soon as I completed my undergrad from a university in India, in December 2007 / January 2008, I relocated back home to my country The United States of America, and lived in Massachusetts for a little less than two years.

In Massachusetts, I worked for a financial software company as a Business Analyst. I had a good life in Massachusetts. My girlfriend at the time who I had started dating during undergrad and was of Indian origin, was also living in Massachusetts at that time. I stayed busy and active, playing tennis on most evenings and working during the day.

After working at the Financial Software company for a little more than one year, I began to realize that I wanted more from my life. I was about 24 years old at the time, and I probably did not consciously realize this at the time, but I was not enjoying being in the Financial Software business. My personal relationship with my girlfriend was also deteriorating.

I resigned from my Business Analyst job in 2009, and soon after, after being in a very emotionally attached relationship with my girlfriend of about 6 and a half to seven years, made the decision to part ways with her.

I remember being very depressed after breaking up with my former girlfriend, but dismissed this feeling as being a temporary jolt in life and moved forward in life.

I decided that maybe Marketing and Business / Entrepreneurship was more my thing in life, and decided to pursue my Masters in Business Administration (MBA). I studied really hard for my GMAT entrance exam, and had a great result.

The application process for MBA schools is a complicated one, and I applied to a few MBA schools. After receiving admission in more than one schools, I decided to enroll in the Full Time MBA program at Southern Methodist University in Dallas, Texas for the Fall 2010 program.

On hindsight, I should have paid more attention to my depression symptoms during the time following me resigning from my Business Analyst job and from breaking up with my former girlfriend. I don't think I handled this life situation as well as I would have liked to, but given that I was in my mid 20's, I guess this is somewhat expected.

I did well above average at my MBA program, and worked really long hours even though the depression symptoms were slowly settling in.

In year 2012, I was a few weeks away from completing my MBA course and graduating with my MBA degree in Marketing and Entrepreneurial Strategy, when tragedy stuck my life. I will not go into too much detail, but long story short, I was diagnosed with Clinical Depression Related Illness and was admitted to the hospital.

What I remember is this – right after I got discharged from the hospital, I started working on my MBA course work: I had worked really hard on a very tough Masters program, and I was not going to give up. I completed the coursework and got my Masters degree soon after.

While I was still taking treatment for my clinical depression related illness, I was determined to try and live a normal and vibrant life.

I relocated to Santa Clara, California in year 2013 to work at a technology company in a Technology Sales job function.

After working at this company for about a year and a bit, I began to realize at a conscious level that technology is not my calling in life. There has to be more to life than this, I felt! I have nothing against the profession of technology, but I realized that while I could be successful and do quite well at this profession, I wanted more from life and wanted a zeal and a passion for life that I was just not feeling working in technology.

American politics had been an area of interest for me at this time in life, and I decided to test the waters.

Now remember this, I was living in one of the most liberal areas of the country, Santa Clara, California. Additionally, almost my entire family, I would say 99.9% of my family at that time (I do not have a family any longer other than my Mom and Dad), was liberal. Furthermore, I used to watch media channels such as CNN, and such Fake News channels moved me further towards the democrat party during this time.

So I thought I was liberal and became a democrat. During some of my speeches in the previous few years, I have called this decision of mine to be a democrat the most horrendous decision of my life.

Anyways, back to my life story: I got an internship in 2015 to work for Hillary Clintons campaign (known to you and me now as Crooked Hillary) in New Hampshire.

All I will say in this: I am very glad and happy that President Donald J. Trump DEFEATED Crooked Hillary soundly in the 2016 Presidential Election and became the 45th President of The United States of America. I believe Crooked Hillary Clinton is one of the worst politicians that America has had, and she should be nowhere near the White House, and never will be.

My memory is a little hazy about this – but I remember switching to the Republican Party at least one or two times from 2016 to 2020. With almost my entire family being liberal at that time, it becomes very challenging and difficult to go against the tide and become a Republican and a Conservative.

Then came year 2020. And life changed. Dramatically. Drastically. And in a GREAT way.

I decided that I wanted to run for elected office. I had a deep desire to serve the country. It was more than a deep desire, it was a calling in life to serve my country. I just was unsure about whether I was a Democrat or a Republican.

I had started getting positively influenced by President Donald J. Trump's books, videos and interviews. However, the inertia about being a democrat was still existing, and

I was also watching Fake News news channels such as CNN and MSNBC.

But there was something about President Donald J. Trump that resonated with me. He actually talked about AMERICA. He actually wanted to help and support AMERICA. And I will be honest, I really love his personality and his ability to communicate his message in a way that is simple and straightforward for regular Americans like you and me to understand and comprehend.

I said to myself – This man is great! He fights for America!

More than being a Republican, I wanted to be a Trump Republican.

After going back and forth on deciding whether I am a Republican or a Democrat, I decided that I will support President Donald J. Trump and I became a Republican.

Now, during this time, I was still undergoing clinical depression related illness and was still taking treatment for this clinical depression related illness, but I decided I was not going to let this stop me from serving my country, The United States of America.

So, I decided to become a Trump Republican and filed my paperwork to officially become a candidate for City Council in Santa Clara, California's District 6 in the 2020 election.

I did not realize this at that time of filing paperwork, but my life had changed forever.

I remember this one incident: I wore a red Make America Great Again hat, in very liberal Santa Clara, California, and went for a walk around the neighborhood. Something felt very right about that hat! I think at that time, I did not realize how much I love America. And with time, my love and solidarity with President Donald J. Trump grew exponentially too.

I remember some people, almost definitely liberal people, looking at me in a not pleasant way on that walk. I also remember that some people seemed to like that I was wearing the MAGA hat. I guess it takes a certain level of courage to wear a MAGA hat in a neighborhood as liberal as the one I was living in.

Few days later, I get a phone call from a gentleman who had become a friend of mine, Peter Kuo. He was at that time the Vice Chair of the California Republican Party.

He asked me to visit him at his office, and I decided to go visit. At his office, he gave me a hat. Actually, I think he gave me two hats. Red hats. They said 'MAKE SANTA CLARA GREAT'.

Peter said, "Will you wear these hats at campaign events?"

I said "Yes, and sometimes even when I am not campaigning. Lets Make Santa Clara Great!".

These hats became quite the thing and quite popular during the campaign, and I got a lot of Press Coverage for my campaign considering it was just my first campaign.

I also remember another incident with Peter Kuo, who is Christian. He and I said a prayer at his office. It was probably the first time I had prayed. After the prayer, I asked Peter, "Please explain to me what this prayer means." Peter said, "Jesus Christ is now alive in you."

I didn't quite realize what this meant at that time. I am not too sure if I started identifying as Christian at that time. But I will tell you this, I remember walking back to my car from his office with a feeling of immense optimism and frankly, peace and calm and serenity that I had NEVER felt before in my life.

Anyways, I campaigned really hard and worked almost all the time, and even when I was not campaigning my mind was on the campaign.

Make Santa Clara Great!

I remember watching a specific President Donald J. Trump video on the internet many times during this time of my life. I have talked about this video in multiple media interviews and also on radio shows and podcasts that I have had the great honor of being a guest on. The video was titled '10 Rules Of Success By President Trump'.

In the video he talks about a few things. He says NEVER GIVE UP, and he says you have to LOVE WHAT YOU DO in your career and in your life.

I said to myself, that is so true! How come I never thought about this?

You see, these advise points are very easy to understand at the right time in life and when you hear it from a person you respect and admire. But it is very difficult to understand and realize these advice points by yourself.

I remember saying this or something like this on my Santa Clara City Council election campaign website:

'Find work in life you love doing, and then do the work with 100% commitment.'

This was just my way of saying: LOVE WHAT YOU DO AND NEVER GIVE UP!

I was endorsed by the Santa Clara County Republican Party, which to me was a nice achievement.

I also want to thank my friend Leim Bui and his friends from the Vietnamese Make America Great Again Group. They went to great lengths to help me during my campaign, whether it was knocking on doors for me or doing a car rally on the streets of Santa Clara, California.

The car rally was really a great and an interesting experience for me. I was actually driving one of the cars in the car rally, and one of the cars in the rally had a huge poster of me wearing the Make Santa Clara Great hat.

After doing really great at a few debates/forums (remember, this was the time of the Covid, also known as the Chinavirus, so the debates/forums happened on video calls), after delivering many speeches and attending events, election day November 3, 2020 arrived.

Now, there was really no practical chance for me to win this election: To my memory the district I was running in had about 17% Republicans. However, I received about 23% of the vote in a 3-person race! This great result surpassed everyone's expectations!

After receiving the election result, I applied to Liberty University in Lynchburg, VA and was granted admission to their Masters Program. I love the fact that Liberty University is a Christian University, and I got baptized at Thomas Road Baptist Church in Lynchburg, VA. While I did not graduate from Liberty University, I completed one course there.

I then relocated to Florida with the hope of getting the opportunity to work for President Trump's 2024 Presidential campaign. However, I decided to run for United States Congress in Florida's 23rd District in the

2024 election as my way to serve our American people and to serve President Trump's America First agenda.

With 6 candidates running in the United States Congress Republican Primary Election, I received close to 2000 votes even though my campaign spent limited money on the campaign.

I then relocated to Iowa. Iowa is the first in the nation caucus election, the people in Iowa are very friendly and incredible and there are many great American farmers in Iowa.

I am currently residing in Arizona, and I am enjoying living here.

HOW I ARRIVED AT THE DECISION THAT I WILL RUN FOR PRESIDENT OF THE UNITED STATES OF AMERICA IN THE 2028 ELECTION

In the previous few years, I have read many books written by President Trump and my favorite is his book THINK BIG. I have read THINK BIG at least 4 to 5 times on audiobook.

In his books and speeches, President Trump always talks about the ability to NEVER GIVE UP and to GO AGAINST THE TIDE and to THINK BIG and to DREAM BIG AND BOLD. He also talks about LOVING OUR USA and SERVING OUR USA. I have over the course of the previous few years tried to imbibe these qualities and attributes in me.

I believe America needs a true American Patriot who will always keep America First and has learnt these qualities and attributes from President Trump's teachings to lead America and continue President Trump's America First legacy from year 2029 and beyond. I also genuinely believe I am following Jesus Christ's path towards serving our country.

I have talked with many great American people and I have taken their advice and thoughts seriously. I believe that the momentum is with me and I have decided that I would like to be that leader for our United States of America and for our great American people.

Over the course of the next few years, I fully anticipate that some people will doubt my experience, politically attack me and work against me to bring me down.

To you the American people I promise this: I love President Trump, I love our great country and I love our great American people and I will face the challenges that I will face head on and FIGHT FIGHT FIGHT for President Donald J. Trump, for our country The United States of America and for YOU our great American people.

With your blessings, encouragement, support and vote, I look forward to winning the Republican Primary Election in year 2028 and then defeating the democrat nominee to win the General Election in November 2028 to help President Trump Make America Great Again, Keep America Great and Save America.

MY FIRST PRESIDENT DONALD J. TRUMP RALLY IN MINDEN, NEVADA

I was a candidate for City Council in Santa Clara's District 6 running as a Republican supporter of President Donald J. Trump in the 2020 election cycle. Per my memory, one of my team members at that time and I got into a conversation about attending President Donald J. Trumps rally that was going to happen live in Minden, Nevada that is only a few hours drive from Santa Clara, California. I believe the rally was on September 13, 2020 just one day prior to my 36th birthday.

My team member and I drove to Minden, Nevada on the day of the rally. As always, tens of thousands of great American patriotic people were standing in long lines to see President Donald J. Trump at his rally.

The rally and President Donald J. Trumps speech was truly passionate and authentic about our great United States of America. This was my first campaign for elected office in my life, and I was slowly but surely getting more and more connected with the love for our great United States of America and love for our President Donald J. Trump that so many patriotic American people share.

I wore a red TRUMP KEEP AMERICA GREAT 2020 shirt at the rally with our great American FLAG on the shirt. I LOVE OUR GREAT AMERICAN FLAG.

That was a great awesome incredible evening.

THE FIRST TIME I MET PRESIDENT DONALD J. TRUMP

On December 1, 2022 I visited President Donald J. Trumps awesome Mar A Lago for the first time. I was there for an event, and heard President Donald J. Trump give an incredible speech in front of many American patriots who love our great United States of America and our President Donald J. Trump. I did not get the opportunity to meet President Donald J. Trump on this day.

However, the next day December 2, 2022 I was attending an event at President Donald J. Trumps golf course Trump International Golf Club in West Palm Beach, Florida.

I initially could not believe it, but President Trump himself was at the golf course playing golf! I was watching him play golf from just outside the Trump International Golf Club restaurant area. He is a great golfer, and it was a fantastic sight. President Trump was driving his own golf cart which I felt is very humble of him, and it was incredible to see about 7 or 8 golf carts following his golf cart: I believe that was The Secret Service following him to protect him.

There were many speeches happening at Trump International Golf Club for the event that I was at, and I remember saying to myself: While I respect the speakers and what they have to say, I am here to try and meet with President Donald J. Trump. So I decided not to attend any of the speeches, or I think to my memory I attended one speech. I decided to spend my time at the restaurant / lounge / breakfast area of the Trump International Golf Club meeting and talking with the many great American people at the Trump International Golf Club, including some members of the Trump International Golf Club.

To be honest, I prefer the one on one interaction with our great American people to learn more about their life story and America First issues that are important to them and talking about how we could Make America Great Again, Keep America Great and Save America and learning from their ideas and feelings for our great United States of America more than listening to speeches anyways.

Here's what I remember: I heard from someone that President Trump has finished playing golf and he is at the Trump International Golf Club restaurant. I actually saw him at the restaurant, but for security reasons I was not allowed to meet him at the restaurant.

A few minutes after that, I was taking a stroll or a quiet walk at the restaurant / lounge / breakfast area of the Trump International Golf Club, when I saw President Donald J. Trump walk out of the restaurant area, and he was right in front of me! I was the only one in the area, and so I walked up to him with calmness and composure and I said to him to my memory these exact words:

PRESIDENT TRUMP I LOVE YOU AND I HAVE RUN FOR ELECTED OFFICE AS A HUGE SUPPORTER OF YOU.

Now President Trump is taller than I am, I believe he is about 6'3 and I am about 5'9 so he sort of looked at me, and said OK as he gave me a friendly fist bump.

I wanted to continue the conversation with him, but many people at the Trump International Golf Club had seen President Trump by this time, and had come to where President Trump and I were standing to meet with him.

I have a few pictures that I have with me that someone took of President Trump and me (along with many other patriotic American people in the picture) but I decided I will not release the pictures on my campaign social media. The reason for this is, I want to meet President Donald J. Trump for a long meeting to get to know him better, and then take a picture or a video with him, and then put it up on campaign social media. I feel that is the honorable thing to do.

So after my quick interaction and friendly fist bump with President Donald J. Trump, he soon went back to the restaurant. His energy and positive aura is incredible and one can really feel his strength and positivity when in his vicinity.

This has been the greatest moment of my life at the time of me writing this book.

I RESPECT OUR AMERICAN PEOPLES RIGHT TO SPEAK ANY LANGUAGE THAT THEY CHOOSE TO SPEAK BUT I LIKE SPEAKING IN ENGLISH. I BELIEVE AMERICA IS AN ENGLISH SPEAKING COUNTRY

I used to speak 3 languages, one of them being English. I say I used to speak 3 languages because since I became a President Donald J. Trump Republican, 99% of the words I say are in ENGLISH. I do not really speak the other 2 languages that I used to speak.

I want to clarify: This is not a policy position, this is just my personal preference. America is (and always will be) a free country and all American people have a right to speak in a language of their preference, I will say, in almost all circumstances. So I respect people who choose to speak in a language that is not English. However, I love speaking in English. English is Americas language and English is my language.

SECTION THREE

THE AMERICA FIRST AGENDA FOR OUR GREAT UNITED STATES OF AMERICA

The first thing I would like to say in this section of my book, is that The Republican Party belongs to President Donald J. Trump. He has completely redefined The Republican Party and it is today the party of our great American hard working patriot.

POSITION AGAINST ILLEGAL IMMIGRATION

During his 2016 Presidential campaign, President Trump highlighted the issue of illegal immigration in our United States of America. For me, this is the issue that is closest to my heart because I believe illegal immigration is destroying our country from within.

From year 2021 to year 2025, under the 'leadership' – or the lack of it – of Crooked Joe Biden and Dumb As A Rock Kamala, approximately 20 Million illegal immigrants entered our country illegally from across the Southern Border. Thousands of these illegal immigrants are convicted murderers, thousands have been criminally charged – this is a fact and the statistics on this have been released by American authorities.

Criminal gangs and cartels such as MS-13 and Tren De Aragua (TdA) have entered our United States of America illegally from across the southern border. These gang members are bad people, they literally cut people up just for fun.

My direct message to any gang member reading this book right now is –

GET THE HELL OUT OF OUR UNITED STATES OF AMERICA. If you don't, America will incarcerate members of your gangs or America will kick out of our country members of your gangs.

Keeping you our American people safe and secure is very important to me, and I am ready to take a bullet for your safety.

I am confident that, to put it mildly, gangs such as MS-13 and Tren De Aragua do not exactly like me for going against them in such a strong way.

To put it realistically, gangs such as MS-13 and Tren De Aragua want me dead, or worse.

And I want to keep it that way.

It means that I am having impact and I am moving the needle towards keeping our United States of America and our American people safe from these criminals and gangs such as MS-13 and Tren De Aragua.

SUPPORT FOR OUR GREAT POLICE, SHERIFFS, ICE, MILITARY, VETERANS, FIRE FIGHTERS AND FIRST RESPONDERS

I am of the strong belief that most Police, Sheriffs, ICE, Military, Veterans, Fire Fighters and First Responders in our great United States of America are great people who love our country and run towards danger to protect civilians and residents they do not even know. I believe this is bravery and courage of the highest level, and we must Defend And Not Defund our Police, Sheriffs, ICE, Military, Veterans, Fire Fighters and First Responders.

The more people in these groups we have, the better and more safer our country will be. I believe that Law and Order is a very important aspect of our United States of America and it is actually in my opinion one of the main fabrics that helps keep our country the greatest country in the world. And I am going to keep fighting to make sure we keep it that way.

I am sharing with you a post I made on campaign social media during my current campaign for President of The United States of America in the 2028 election as a Republican supporter of our President Donald J.

Trump. I believe the campaign social media post is self explanatory:

UNSUNG HEROES: POLICE, SHERIFFS, ICE, MILITARY, VETERANS, FIRE FIGHTERS, FIRST RESPONDERS

As a candidate running for President of The United States of America as a Republican supporter of President Donald J. Trump, and as a former City Council and US Congress candidate as a President Trump supporter, I have received some recognition via a little bit of Press Coverage and Media Attention, and have been able to courageously talk about my positions against crime, gangs such as TREN de ARAGUA, MS-13 and illegal immigration.

However I genuinely believe that our POLICE, SHERIFFS, ICE, MILITARY, VETERANS, FIRE FIGHTERS, FIRST RESPONDERS are our UNSUNG HEROES. They do not always get the recognition they deserve, and are more courageous than most people running for elected office including me. At the same time, I feel they are poorly compensated from a salary perspective in many jurisdictions in our country.

There are many other professions that start with huge salaries, and their job descriptions do not require them to risk their lives for our American people on a daily basis. While I have nothing against huge salaries for these other professions, I believe our POLICE, SHERIFFS, ICE,

MILITARY, VETERANS, FIRE FIGHTERS, FIRST RESPONDERS should be better compensated.

I have already made a campaign promise that I will support President Trump's America First agenda 100% until Nov 2028, and that after Nov 2028 if I am elected President of The USA I will make decisions for our USA keeping America First and our American People First.

I will keep this (and all) my promises, and in line with my promises I will push for and promote the idea of better and just compensation for our UNSUNG HEROES if I am elected 48th President of The USA in Nov 2028, and will happily talk about it during my Presidential campaign.

This is my campaign promise to you our great American people.

AMERICA IS TRUMP COUNTRY.

Gary Barve

I am also sharing another campaign social media post with you. I believe the campaign social media post is self explanatory:

America has spent over $100 BILLION on Ukraine in the Russia–Ukraine conflict. For a fraction of this amount, America can GET EVERY HOMELESS GREAT AMERICAN VETERAN OFF THE STREETS!

I want ZERO VETERAN HOMELESSNESS, ZERO VETERAN JOBLESSNESS AND COMPLETE MENTAL HEALTH SERVICES FOR OUR GREAT AMERICAN VETERANS.

I have made a campaign promise that I will support President Trump's America First agenda 100% until Nov 2028, and if I am elected President of The USA in Nov 2028 I will make decisions for our country keeping America First and our American People First. I will keep all my promises.

I am going to talk about this initiative with personnel who worked with President Trump's campaign.

I will support this initiative if I get elected the 48th President of The USA. This is a Campaign Promise.

Our great American Veterans put their lives on the line to serve YOU. Now WE SERVE AND SUPPORT OUR GREAT AMERICAN VETERANS.

Gary Barve

THE AMERICAN ECONOMY: TARIFFS AND LOW TAXES AND LIMITED GOVERNMENT

I believe in Tariffs. I believe Tariffs is the most beautiful word in the world of Economics. Some Economists say that Tariffs will not work too well, however President Donald J. Trump believes in Tariffs and I have learnt a lot about Tariffs from President Donald J. Trump and I believe strongly in Tariffs.

Tariffs are a great way to keep businesses and companies in America and to bring businesses and companies that are outside our great United States of America back into our United States of America so that jobs and employment opportunities are created here in our country for our American people.

Here's how Tariffs work:

For example, lets say there is an American company, say a car manufacturing company or any other company, that wants to manufacture its product outside our United States of America, say in Mexico, and then bring that product back to our United States of America and then sell that product within our United States of America.

One of the reasons businesses or companies do this, is because they want to take advantage of the cheap labor that is available in some foreign countries that allows the businesses or companies to manufacture or build their product at a lower cost.

They then bring this product that they manufacture at a lower cost because of the cheap labor, into our United States of America and sell that product to you our great American people. The cheap labor in countries such as Mexico where they manufacture their product, allows these companies or businesses to have higher margins and hence they make a bigger or larger profit.

Now I will say this confidently: I want American companies to make a large profit. I want American companies to make a lot of money and be great American companies. But I do not want this to happen at the cost and expense of YOU our great American people, because when companies and businesses build their product outside our United States of America, they are NOT going to hire YOU our great American people! They are going to end up hiring the people in the foreign country where they manufacture or build their product.

Here is the solution, and you are going to love the solution: TARRIFS!

Wherever practical, if I get elected President of The United States of America in the 2028 election as a

Republican supporter of our President Donald J. Trump, I will apply a 10% tariff, or a 25% tariff, or a 50% tariff, or a 100% tariff or a 1000% tariff on all products or goods that businesses and companies manufacture outside our great United States of America, and bring into our United States of America.

Know what this does?

If the correct amount of tariff is applied to the business or company manufacturing their product outside our United States of America and bringing that product into our United States of America, it becomes ECONOMICALLY UNVIABLE for the business or company to manufacture their product outside our country and then bring it back into our country and then sell it within our country to you our great American people. The math no longer works out for the business or company.

Guess what this does?

The business or company decides to now manufacture or build their product WITHIN our great United States of America, because when the business or company builds their product within our great United States of America, there is NO TARIFF. So the business or company now finds it economically effective to build or manufacture their product within our country.

Guess what this means?

Jobs and employment opportunities are now created in AMERICA!

OUR AMERICAN PEOPLE GET HIRED.

OUR AMERICAN PEOPLE GET JOBS.

And we create a flourishing economy for our country.

And that is what I want.

The business or company WINS.

Our American people WIN.

AND AMERICA WINS.

But wait, there is more:

President Donald J. Trump has said that if the business or company manufactures or builds their product within our great United States of America, the tax will go down from the current approximately 21% to approximately 15%. That is a great incentive for businesses or companies to come back into out United States of America, or better yet, not leave our United States of America in the first place.

So this is how tariffs work.

I look at Tariffs as a weapon. It is a weapon that keeps businesses, companies, jobs and employment opportunities within our United States of America and helps create a thriving American economy. AMERICA FIRST!

Remember this, under President Donald J. Trumps first term as President of The United States of America, America had the greatest economy ever in the history of our country for all Americans including Caucasian Americans or White Americans, African Americans or Black Americans, Hispanic Americans, Men, Women.

The additional way to achieve this great economy is low taxes.

When America has low taxes, two things happen: Our American people, our great American worker, gets to keep more of his or her money.

Remember this, this is YOUR hard earned money. YOU work 40 hours, 50 hours, 60 hours a week for your money. For your salary. Do you really want to give away a large amount of your salary that you work so hard for, to the government so that the government can spend a lot of it on frivolous activities and initiatives that you may not really believe in?

Ask yourself the question: Why would you or any American want this?

I will give you an example. Lets say you are a great American Farmer. Or a great American Coal Mine Worker. Or a great American Taxi Cab driver. Or a great

American Bartender. Or a great American Police, Sheriff, ICE member, Military member, Veteran, Fire Fighter or First Responder. Or a great American Oil & Gas worker. Or lets say you work at a Fast Food restaurant.

You work 50 hours in a week, and you make for the sake of this example $20 per hour. That's a total of $1000 that YOU EARNED with YOUR HARD WORK so that you could support YOU AND YOUR FAMILY.

Do you really want to give a LARGE amount of this $1000 to the GOVERNMENT in the form of a large TAX so that some elected official can spend it on an initiative that you could be completely against?

How does this make sense for you our great American worker?

I want YOU to keep a LARGE PORTION of the $1000 you made in the week. YOU should decide where you want to spend YOUR money. NOT the government. YOU get more control when there are low taxes.

And this is what I Gary Barve, President Donald J. Trump and President Donald J. Trumps Republican Party would want to see happen, and hence we support low taxes and limited Government.

We want our AMERICAN PEOPLE to be POWERFUL and STRONG.

Now I will say this: At the time of writing this book, I feel that some amount of low tax is required to keep our country moving along smoothly. And so I say I believe in low taxes.

The democrat party wants to INCREASE TAXES so that the democrat elected officials have more money to play with: more of YOUR MONEY to play with.

Why would you support this? Perhaps the democrat party wants to keep the logic I mentioned in the previous few paragraphs away from you so that they get to keep your money.

Think about it, my fellow American.

SUPPORT FOR OUR GREAT AMERICAN FARMERS, COAL MINE WORKERS, OIL AND GAS WORKERS, TRUCKERS AND MOTORCYCLE RIDERS, BAR TENDERS, RESTAURANT WORKERS AND FOR ALL OUR HARD WORKING LAW ABIDING PATRIOTIC FREEDOM LOVING AMERICAN MEN AND WOMEN

I love our great American Farmers, coal mine workers, oil and gas workers, truckers and motorcycle riders, bar tenders, restaurant workers and really all our hard working law abiding patriotic freedom loving American Men and Women. These jobs and professions are tough and difficult professions that require immense hard work.

I also feel that the American people in these groups: American farmers, coal mine workers, oil and gas workers, truckers and motorcycle riders, bar tenders, restaurant workers and so many other hard working professions are very PATRIOTIC about our United States of America. You HAVE to LOVE our United States of America. And the people in the groups I just mentioned really love our United States of America and they love our great AMERICAN FLAG.

I also feel that most people or many people in these professions I mentioned are simple people, and I say this in a very positive way. But because I feel that they are simple people, many politicians and bureaucrats take advantage of the American patriots in these groups I mentioned. And I do not like that.

I Gary Barve will fight for all the Patriotic American people mentioned here.

I WILL FIGHT FOR OUR HARD WORKING LAW ABIDING FREEDOM LOVING PATRIOTIC AMERICAN MEN AND WOMEN WHO LOVE OUR UNITED STATES OF AMERICA AND WANT TO LIVE THE AMERICAN DREAM.

I also believe that when it comes to farming, China should not be allowed to own any farmland in our United States of America. This is a campaign promise: If I get elected President of The United States of America in the 2028 election as a Republican supporter of our President Donald J. Trump, I will not allow China to own any farmland in our United States of America.

I have mentioned more about this in the Foreign Policy section a few pages further in this book.

DRILLING FOR OIL AND GAS IN OUR GREAT UNITED STATES OF AMERICA

I support drilling for Oil and Gas domestically within our United States of America. President Donald J. Trump mentioned during his successful and victorious 2024 election campaign for President of The United States of America that he will support drilling for Oil and Gas on Day 1 of his second term in The White House. I am 100% in support of that too.

Why does the democrat party not support drilling for Oil and Gas domestically in our United States of America? The democrat party's position makes NO SENSE.

Here's why the democrat party's position makes NO SENSE:

The democrat party says they do not support drilling for Oil and Gas within our United States of America because it pollutes the environment and negatively affects the environment. But under the democrat party administration, America then buys Oil and Gas from foreign countries such as Venezuela, where drilling for Oil and Gas is multiple times more environmentally unfriendly than drilling for Oil and Gas domestically in our United States of America. America is one of the cleanest if not THE cleanest countries in the world when it comes to drilling for Oil and Gas! Furthermore, there is a literally zero percent chance that the entire world will suddenly stop drilling for Oil and Gas and go electric instead, international dynamics will not allow this to happen.

So essentially what the democrat party is saying is, let other foreign countries take the economic benefit of drilling for Oil and Gas in their countries, while America buys the Oil and Gas from these foreign countries leading to economic inflation and higher price of Oil and Gas in our United States of America.

So you see what happens with this democrat party policy right?

The world gets the negative effects of drilling for Oil and Gas anyways, and America and our great American people suffer from higher price of Oil and Gas.

Do you like this deal? How does that make sense?

Also, America has more Oil and Gas than any other country on earth. President Donald J. Trump calls it Liquid Gold.

There are many advantages to drilling for Oil and Gas domestically within our United States of America.

The main advantage is it reduces the cost of Oil and Gas in our United States of America for our American people. And this reduces economic inflation.

Remember this: Under President Donald J. Trumps first term as President of The United States of America, the price of gas in many areas of our country was as low or perhaps even lower than $1.87 per gallon.

Under the democrat party administration our American people in places such as California were at times paying about $8 per gallon or more!

As they say, the proof is in the pudding: President Donald J. Trump and his Republican Party policy about drilling for Oil and Gas domestically works!

Also, here's how America reduces economic inflation when we drill for Oil and Gas domestically:

When America drills for Oil and Gas domestically, the cost of the entire supply chain goes down: construction, manufacturing, shipping, transportation, raw materials – these costs go down and that reduces the consumer cost of product, that is, it reduces the price you pay for groceries such as bread and butter and eggs and milk in the market.

So essentially, I am proving this to any doubters:

Drilling for Oil and Gas domestically within our United States of America makes no difference to the pollution level in the world – in fact, since America is the cleanest producer of Oil and Gas in the world the pollution level actually reduces comparatively if America drills for Oil and Gas domestically – and this also reduces the price you pay at the Gas Station for Oil and Gas and reduces economic inflation across the country too.

GAS VEHICLES AND ELECTRIC VEHICLES IN AMERICA:

I want to talk about the issue of car manufacturing in America and the democrat party's policy mandate that all cars or a large percentage of cars in America should be electric.

This mandate makes no sense. America is not some sort of a dictatorship where the government mandates that our American people must buy only electric cars.

I want our American people to have the option of buying a gas vehicle if that is what they prefer – and a large majority of Americans prefer this – and if they want to buy an electric vehicle then that option should be available for them too. Our American people should decide the car they want to purchase. Not the government!

AMERICAN EDUCATION

American education MUST be PATRIOTIC education. I believe we must instill a feeling of LOVE FOR AMERICA within our young children and young students.

A American people that loves the country makes a STRONG AND POWERFUL United States of America.

Men should NOT compete in women's sports.

Transgender surgeries should not be allowed for children in America.

America must fight against the Critical Race Theory or the CRT. I believe the Critical Race Theory or The CRT has been designed by the democrat party to divide our country racially. I also believe that the Critical Race Theory or The CRT has been designed by the democrat party to make Caucasian people or White people feel like they are Oppressors or White Supremacists just for being White – and I can say this with some level of freedom as a person of color as some people like to call it.

I will say this: I have been a member of The Trump Republican Party for many years. There is ZERO RACISM in The Trump Republican Party, and President Donald J. Trump is a NOT RACIST person.

We are not White American, we are not Black American and we are not Brown American, we are American and ALL LIVES MATTER.

FIRST AMENDMENT: FREEDOM OF SPEECH

I believe the First Amendment is one of the ways our great United States of America remains a free country. Very important!

SECOND AMENDMENT: THE RIGHT TO KEEP AND BEAR ARMS

I am a big supporter of The Second Amendment, the right to keep and bear arms.

I support the Second Amendment for few reasons. I am mentioning three reasons here:

First, the Second Amendment is in the United States Constitution, so it is protected.

Second, let me give you an example. On October 7, 2023 the terrorist organization Hamas viciously attacked the people of Israel. Israel is Americas friend and ally and I am a big supporter of Israel. However, I believe that if Israel would have had the Second Amendment in their country just like we Americans have the Second Amendment in our country, there would have been a substantially different result in Israel on October 7, 2023. I want to make sure that an October 7, 2023 does not happen on our land in our great United States of America.

Third, I believe the Second Amendment gives our law abiding American people the ability to protect themselves and gives them the ability to do self defense when required.

FOREIGN POLICY

The first thing I would mention to you our great American people, is that remember this: There were no new wars under President Donald J. Trump during his first term in the White House as the 45th President of The United States of America.

I believe the way President Donald J. Trump managed to achieve this, is he built successful working relationships with leaders of the world such as President Xi of China, Putin of Russia, Zelensky of Ukraine and Kim Jong Un of North Korea but at the same time he projected American strength.

As a result, these leaders of the world respected President Donald J. Trump, and they still respect President Donald J. Trump, but they also respected our country The United States of America. This respect for our country from the world helped keep the world at peace. In fact, President Donald J. Trump also decimated 100% of the ISIS in a matter of about 5 weeks.

Like President Trump, I am also a big believer in Peace Through Strength. I feel that the President of The United States of America's personality, the way and manner of communicating, sense of timing and gut instinct along with heart for America plays a big factor in achieving the very complicated but effective art of Peace Through Strength.

The Russia Ukraine conflict and the Israel Hamas conflict would never have happened under President Donald J. Trumps leadership. It happened under Crooked Joe Biden and Dumb As A Rock Kamala's weak and ineffective 'leadership', or the lack of it.

President Trump has said that while he is America First, he wants the killing to stop in the Russia Ukraine conflict and that he will negotiate peace between Russia and Ukraine very fast.

About the Israel Hamas conflict, I mentioned earlier that I am a big supporter of Israel. I believe Israel is Americas friend and ally. Hamas is a terrorist organization and the October 7, 2023 attack by Hamas against Israel was horrific. I want all hostages including all American hostages to be released immediately, and I am confident that President Donald J. Trump will do everything in his capacity to achieve this as the 47th President of The United States of America.

China is obviously a communist country, and is not a friend of America to put it mildly. I will say this – President Xi of China is a smart man and a strong man, he rules his Chinese Communist Party with an iron fist. However, he loves China. President Trump and I love our great country The United States of America.

If I get elected President of The United States of America in the 2028 election as a Republican supporter of President Donald J. Trump, China will respect our country and President Xi will respect me as President of The United States of America, and I will always keep America First.

I am making a campaign promise that if I am elected President of The United States of America in November 2028, I will not allow China to own any farmland in our great United States of America. Our American farmers are great people and they are getting ripped off by China. Owning farmland is also China's way of gaining control over American land. China has also begun acquiring land near military bases in America, and I will put an end to this.

Furthermore, America should not allow China to own critical infrastructure in our great United States of America, such as natural resources, energy and technology.

Chinese spies are in America, and America will put an end to this espionage.

ELECTION INTEGRITY

Election Integrity is a very important America First agenda issue. We want fair and just elections in our country. I support paper ballots, same day election, voter ID and signature verification. This will ensure America has free fair and just elections going forward.

The 2020 Presidential election was stolen by the democrat party from President Donald J. Trump and from his Republican Party. I believe President Trump won the 2020 election in a landslide.

Remember this, President Trump got more votes in the 2020 election than any sitting President ever. Crooked Joe Biden on the other hand used Covid, also called as the Chinavirus, as an excuse to stay in his basement and hide his tremendous inabilities by not really campaigning.

The democrat party also used Covid or Chinavirus as an excuse to exploit Mail In Ballots and cheat in the elections.

The 2024 Presidential election was a tremendous WIN for President Donald J. Trump. It was Too Big To Rig, and he won all 7 battleground states by huge margins against Dumb As A Rock Kamala.

LEGAL AS IN LAWFUL IMMIGRATION

I support legal as in lawful immigration that supports the American economy, supports our American worker and supports American values and American way of life.

SECTION FOUR

As I mentioned earlier in my book, I am running for President of The United States of America in the 2028 election because I love President Donald J. Trump, I love our country the greatest country in the world The United States of America and I love our great American people. I want to help President Donald J. Trump Make America Great Again, Keep America Great and Save America.

I have made a campaign promise that I will support President Donald J. Trump's America First agenda mentioned on my campaign website 100% until November 2028, and then if I get the great honor of being elected President of The United States of America in the 2028 election, I will continue President Donald J. Trump's legacy by always making decisions for our country keeping you our American people first, and keeping our country, America First.

I have been supporting President Donald J. Trump's America First agenda for many years, long before he became the Republican nominee in the 2024 Presidential election and long before he became President Elect by winning the election for President of The United States of America on November 5, 2024.

I want to share two stories with you.

First Story:

President Donald J. Trump announced on November 15, 2022 that he will run for President of The United States of America in the 2024 election cycle. I remember watching the announcement speech on TV and I said to myself and I said this to a lot of people: President Donald J. Trump is a big Christian, Jesus Christ is with President Donald J. Trump, and President Donald J. Trump will win the election and he will Save America.

Now, I want to say this very strongly: I respect all religions. However, I am Christian and I believe in Jesus Christ as my Lord and Savior.

So, President Donald J. Trump's campaign moved forward, and we all know what happened: Indictment 1, Indictment 2, Indictment 3 and Indictment 4 against President Donald J. Trump because of the political weaponization of The Department of Justice skewed against President Donald J. Trump, President Donald J. Trump supporters and candidates supporting President Donald J. Trump because of the corrupt democrat party.

And I kept saying the same thing: President Donald J. Trump is a big Christian, Jesus Christ is with President Donald J. Trump, and President Donald J. Trump will win the election and he will Save America.

Then there were assassination attempts against President Donald J. Trump: The first assassination attempt on July 13, 2024 was so close to being an even worse day than it was, it was a matter of 1/8th of an inch.

And I kept saying the same thing: President Donald J. Trump is a big Christian, Jesus Christ is with President Donald J. Trump, and President Donald J. Trump will win the election and he will Save America.

And then November 5, 2024 arrived and President Donald J. Trump WON the election in a landslide, winning all 7 Battleground States against Dumb As A Rock Kamala. The election was not even close, and it was truly TOO BIG TO RIG!

All this to say that I believe in President Donald J. Trump more than just about anyone else in the country. I believe by winning the election on November 5, 2024 he has already Saved America, and he will continue to Make America Great Again, Keep America Great and Save America as The 47th President of The United States of America.

My statements about my belief that Jesus Christ is with President Donald J. Trump are documented in many social media posts and in a recorded video speech that I delivered just minutes after the horrific July 13, 2024 assassination attempt against President Donald J. Trump.

Second Story:

On July 13, 2024 I was at a Vietnamese Make America Great Again event in Florida. I was at that time running for United States Congress in Florida District 23 as a Republican supporter of President Donald J. Trump.

I was actually in conversation with a candidate for Sheriff at the Vietnamese Make America Great Again event, when the actual horrific assassination attempt against President Donald J. Trump happened, and the candidate for Sheriff is the one who broke the news to me – he said to me, Gary, President Trump has been shot.

I was devastated when I heard him say that, because I love President Donald J. Trump, but even in that moment of devastation, I remember saying to the candidate for Sheriff: President Donald J. Trump is ok right, nothing can happen to him. I said this because I genuinely believe that Jesus Christ is with President Donald J. Trump, Jesus Christ is with our country and Jesus Christ is with our great American people.

So, I went on stage at the Vietnamese Make America Great Again event on July 13, 2024 just minutes after the horrific assassination attempt against President Donald J. Trump, I completely modified my speech, and said the following 3 things to show my love, support and solidarity with President Donald J. Trump:

First, my direct message to the criminals, gangs, cartels such as MS-13, to the drug dealers, drug smugglers and human traffickers is this: Your brutal reign of terror in our great United States of America will come to an end on November 5, 2024 when President Donald J. Trump will WIN the election and he will once again shut down the Southern Border, build the wall, stop catch and release, stop asylum fraud and designate all foreign cartels in our country as foreign terrorist organizations, and he will once again MAKE AMERICA GREAT AGAIN!

Second, my direct message to the criminals is this: If you fire a bullet at President Donald J. Trump, or if you fire a bullet at me fighting for my and our great United States of America, I believe and I am sure President Donald J. Trump also believes: It is not our responsibility to duck from the bullet, it is the bullets responsibility to miss us.

And Third, I believe Jesus Christ is with President Donald J. Trump, Jesus Christ is with our country and Jesus Christ is with our great American people and President Donald J. Trump will win the election on November 5, 2024 and he will Make America Great Again.

This video is posted on my campaign social media with the timestamp, and it is also on my campaign website.

And finally, I would like to share with you that I love President Donald J. Trump for many reasons, and I would like to share with you two of those reasons:

First, President Donald J. Trump is fighting for our country in a way that no man has fought for our country before. He has infinite faith and infinite love for our great American people. I take immense inspiration from the fight that President Donald J. Trump has shown and continues to show for our great United States of America and for our great American people.

The second reason for my love for President Donald J. Trump is more personal to me: I shared with you in my book that I was diagnosed with a clinical depression related illness many years back. While I have now made a complete recovery from my battle with clinical depression related illness and I take no treatment now, I certainly struggled with the illness for many years. There was a point in my life many years back when I was completely down and out, and I was looking for inspiration.

I started reading President Donald J. Trump's books, and watched his interviews, speeches and videos. There is one particular video from President Donald J. Trump that truly inspired me, titled 10 Rules Of Success By President Donald J. Trump. In the video, he talks about tremendous wisdom such as Never Give Up and Go Against The Tide.

I found his personality and the manner in which he gave the advice to be very powerful and yet simple. I loved the video so much that I have watched it probably 100 times.

I got inspired by President Donald J. Trump via his books, speeches, videos and interviews to not just fight for my life, but to fight for my country, the greatest country in the world, The United States of America.

So I will complete SECTION FOUR of my book by saying this:

I love you President Donald J. Trump. When the 2020 election was stolen from you by the corrupt democrat party, many people deserted you. Many people turned against you. Many people tried to destroy you. At that time, I had no idea that you will run for President of The United States of America in the 2024 election. I am confident that you know that many people believed you will never run for President of The United States of America in the 2024 election, and I am confident that you know that many people thought you will never become President of The United States of America again.

I disagreed with these people. I stood with you through thick and thin, through the ups and the downs, and fought for you in a way that no man has fought for you before.

And so I say this to the 47th President of The United States of America President Donald J. Trump:

There is only one reason why I did this. I love you.

In Christ,
Gary Barve

SECTION FIVE: CAMPAIGN SOCIAL MEDIA POSTS

In this section of my book, I am including some posts that I have made on my campaign social media that I feel you will find interesting, informative and perhaps even some- what controversial.

My campaign website is <u>www.GaryBarveForAmerica.</u> <u>com</u> and links to my campaign social media are avail- able from my campaign website.

Nikki 'Democrat Running As A Republican' Birdbrain Haley is DISLOYAL to President Donald J. Trump and our great USA.

She was appointed US Ambassador to the UN by President Donald J. Trump.

She said on camera she will not run against President Donald J. Trump.

And she then decided to show her gratitude by running against President Donald J. Trump. And she lost soundly to President Donald J. Trump.

AMERICA—If Nikki 'Democrat Running As A Republican' Birdbrain Haley cannot be LOYAL to the man who supported her so much, President Donald J. Trump, do you think she will be LOYAL to you, our great American people? Think about it.

Gary Barve

Florida Governor Ron DeSanctimonious is along with Nikki 'Democrat Running As A Republican' Birdbrain Haley the MOST DISLOYAL PERSON in America.

President Donald J. Trump endorsed Ron DeSanctimonious for Governor, when Ron DeSanctimonious was losing the election and was dropping like a rock in the polls.

As a direct result of the endorsement from President Donald J. Trump, Ron DeSanctimonious became Florida Governor.

Ron DeSanctimonious decided to show his gratitude by running against President Donald J. Trump in the 2024 Presidential Primary Election, and enjoyed a massive defeat.

AMERICA—If Ron DeSanctimonious cannot be LOYAL to the man who supported him so much, President Donald J. Trump, do you think he will be LOYAL to you, our great American people? Think about it.

Gary Barve

My advice for Nikki 'Democrat Running As A Republican' Birdbrain Haley—Join the democrat party at your earliest possible convenience.

Many of your 'supporters' in the 2024 Presidential Primary Election were liberal / democrats, and you have a better shot at becoming the nominee on the democrat side.

While you are at it, ask Ron DeSanctimonious to join you on the democrat side, though I think he will decline your invitation.

Both you and Ron DeSanctimonious are VERY DISLOYAL to President Donald J. Trump and our great USA. President Donald J. Trump supported you, and you still decided to run against him.

Your DISLOYALTY will be appreciated by the democrat elected officials.

Gary Barve

Texas Senator Ted Cruz is a real beauty. He used underhanded tactics to try and secure votes in the 2016 Presidential Primary Election, and earned himself the nickname LYIN' TED.

LYIN' TED's interviews on TV come across as monotone and boring, and LYIN' TED enjoyed a massive defeat against President Donald J. Trump in the 2016 Republican Primary Election.

LYIN' TED has limited to zero personality.

Gary Barve

◇◇

Kari Lake has a moderate to low level of charm—just enough to make sure that she suffered massive defeats in 2022 and 2024 in her statewide election in Arizona.

Remember this -

President Donald J. Trump WON Arizona in the 2024 election by a MASSIVE about 5 Percentage Points against Kamala.

Kari Lake LOST Arizona in the 2024 election by a MASSIVE about 2 Percentage Points against her democrat opponent.

What went wrong Kari?

Kari Lake does not have what it takes to WIN and MAKE AMERICA GREAT AGAIN, KEEP AMERICA GREAT AND SAVE AMERICA.

Gary Barve

Opportunistic RINO Weak Little Vivek Ram-A-Swamy is NOT a loyal supporter of President Donald J. Trump.

My question to Opportunistic RINO Weak Little Vivek Ram-A-Swamy is this—if you are a LOYAL supporter of President Donald J. Trump, why did you run against him?

When you run against someone for political office, you are looking to defeat that person. Also you are looking to potentially destroy the opponent if it's the right thing to do.

While Opportunistic RINO Weak Little Vivek Ram-A-Swamy and his team were plotting against President Donald J. Trump, I loyally supported President Donald J. Trump.

Also, while I respect all religions, I am Christian and I strongly believe that Jesus Christ is Lord and Savior. I strongly believe that Jesus Christ is with President Donald J. Trump, Jesus Christ is with our USA and Jesus Christ is with our great American people.

Gary Barve

I think at this time that Texas Governor Greg Abbott is a decent guy but I will say this to Greg Abbott–It's Game On if you decide to run for President against me in the 2028 election.

Gary Barve

◇◇

Awkward Inauthentic RINO Glenn Youngkin is a RINO (Republican In Name Only). He did not endorse President Donald J. Trump for a LONG time in the 2024 Presidential Election.

Awkward Inauthentic RINO Glenn Youngkin also actively considered running against President Donald J. Trump in the 2024 Presidential Election.

Awkward Inauthentic RINO Glenn Youngkin is too political and plastic and lacks genuineness.

MAGA WILL REJECT AWKWARD INAUTHENTIC RINO GLENN YOUNGKIN.

Gary Barve

❖❖

Florida Congressman Byron Donald's has a moderately decent personality, but have you noticed that he does not have a ready smile and lacks charm?

Gary Barve

Chris 'Colossal RINO' Christie has The Trump Derangement Syndrome. His 2024 Presidential Campaign which was a massive failure was all about 'Chris Christie is against President Donald J. Trump'.

MAGA does not support Chris 'Colossal RINO' Christie.

Gary Barve

◇◇

Mike Pence BETRAYED President Donald J. Trump and our great American MAGA patriots. Mike Pence should have sent the votes back to the states.

Mike Pence hardly registered on the polls in the 2024 Presidential Primary Election, and had a zero chance of winning or coming anywhere near the remote possibility of winning.

My message to Mike Pence is—Follow Jesus Christ in practice, and love Him and love our great USA.

Mike Pence is not MAGA.

And America has realized this.

Gary Barve

Chris 'Colossal RINO' Christie, Nikki 'Democrat Running As A Republican' Birdbrain Haley and Ted Cruz are VIBRATING AT THE WRONG FREQUENCY when it comes to MAGA and our USA.

Same can be said about Ron DeSanctimonious, Opportunistic RINO Weak Little Vivek Ram-A-Swamy, Glenn 'Awkward RINO' Youngkin, Byron Donalds, Kari Lake, Greg Abbot, Mike Pence and many more.

AMERICA IS TRUMP COUNTRY.

Gary Barve 🇺🇸

<><><><><><><><><><><><><><><><><><><><><><><><><><><><><><><><><><><><><><><><>

Ron DeSanctimonious, Glenn 'Awkward Inauthentic RINO' Youngkin and Opportunistic RINO Weak Little Vivek Ram-A-Swamy have the personality of a TIN CAN, that means they have an unattractive bad weak and frail personality!

When you watch them speak, you KNOW that there is something lacking. That unique almost undefinable yet very obvious I AM PRESIDENT OF THE UNITED STATES OF AMERICA Presidential Quality that President Donald J. Trump has is not there with Ron DeSanctimonious, Glenn 'Awkward Inauthentic RINO' Youngkin and Opportunistic RINO Weak Little Vivek Ram-A-Swamy. And YOU KNOW IT!

Gary Barve

Mike Pence has the personality of a PINHEAD. No charm, no warmth and almost zero registered on the polls in the 2024 Presidential Primary Election.

Gary Barve

◇◇

I believe Kamala Harris could run in the 2028 democrat Presidential Primary Election.

As I have said many times in the previous weeks and months, Kamala is DUMB AS A ROCK!

She is an EMPTY SUIT, which means she is an unremarkable person. Her embarrassing word salads make no sense.

Kamala is also very INCOMPETENT and lacks ability. This was proven on Nov 5, 2024 when President Donald J. Trump strongly DEFEATED KAMALA in ALL 7 BATTLEGROUND STATES one after the other to make the greatest political comeback in the history of our USA.

Kamala and her Kamala Democrat Party are destroying our great USA.

Now President Donald J. Trump and our incredible MAGA Patriots will MAKE AMERICA GREAT AGAIN, KEEP AMERICA GREAT AND SAVE AMERICA.

Gary Barve

Gavin Newsom also known as GAVIN NEWSCUM is the WORST GOVERNOR IN AMERICA. His California Last policies are destroying California.

Businesses and people are leaving California in numbers.

There is illegal immigration in California because of GAVIN NEWSCUM's support for open borders and Sanctuary Cities.

Also, have you looked at Gavin NEWSCUM's HORRIFIC HAIR and the amount of Hair Gel he seems to put on it? I believe this itself should be an IMMEDIATE DISQUALIFIER for GAVIN NEWSCUM to run for President or be President—and I say that tongue in cheek, but MAGA WILL NOT ALLOW GAVIN 'HAIR GEL' NEWSCUM TO GET ANYWHERE NEAR THE WHITE HOUSE BECAUSE AMERICA WILL NEVER RUN ON GAVIN NEWSCUM'S CALIFORNIA LAST AND AMERICA LAST POLICIES!

Gary Barve

I hope either GAVIN 'HAIR GEL' NEWSCUM or DUMB AS A ROCK KAMALA become the democrat nominees in the 2028 Presidential Election.

If I get the great honor of becoming the Republican Party Nominee in the 2028 Presidential Primary Election, I WILL ENJOY DEFEATING GAVIN 'HAIR GEL' NEWSCUM or DUMB AS A ROCK KAMALA.

Even better—Let GAVIN 'HAIR GEL' NEWSCUM or DUMB AS A ROCK KAMALA be on the democrat ticket together.

Defeating BOTH GAVIN 'HAIR GEL' NEWSCUM AND DUMB AS A ROCK KAMALA will be more enjoyable!

Gary Barve

◇◇◇

Has anyone realized that the democrat party or as I call it The Kamala Democrat Party has a WEAK BENCH of potential 2028 Presidential Election candidates?

Gary Barve

CROOKED HILLARY, POCAHONTAS ELIZABETH WARREN, SOCIALIST BERNIE SANDERS, PETE BOOT-EDGE-EDGE— WILL YOU RUN FOR PRESIDENT IN 2028 on the Kamala Democrat Party side?

GO FOR IT! I WILL ENJOY RUNNING AGAINST YOU AND DEFEATING YOU!

Gary Barve

I AM READY TO TAKE A BULLET FOR MY COUNTRY.

I AM READY TO GO TO JAIL FOR MY COUNTRY.

I have strongly and fearlessly fought against criminals, gangs, cartels such as MS-13, drug dealers, drug smugglers, human traffickers via my speeches and campaign advertisements.

I have fought against political weaponization of the DOJ skewed against President Trump, President Trump supporters and candidates supporting President Trump by the corrupt Joe Biden-Kamala Harris democrat party.

And I will continue to fight for YOU our great American people, for President Trump and for our great nation.

I am humbly asking you to support my campaign for President of The USA in the 2028 election as a Republican supporter of President Trump.

If you are able to, please consider making a campaign contribution via the Donate/Contribute Button on my campaign website.

Campaign website is **www.GaryBarveForAmerica.com**

Thank you for your support. MAGA!

Gary Barve

◇◇◇

On Nov 5, 2024 President Donald J. Trump will win the election, and we will KICK OUT OF OUR COUNTRY OR INCARCERATE members of criminal gangs such as Venezuelan gang TREN DE ARAGUA (TdA) and MS-13.

America: If you elect me Gary Barve the 48th President of The United States of America I promise you today that I will fearlessly and strongly continue President Donald J. Trump's legacy and Keep America Safe.

My message to criminal gangs such as Venezuelan gang TREN DE ARAGUA (TdA) and MS-13 is straightforward— GET THE HELL OUT OF OUR UNITED STATES OF AMERICA!

Gary Barve

SECRET SERVICE AND LAW ENFORCEMENT—PROTECT PRESIDENT DONALD J. TRUMP WITH EVERYTHING YOU'VE GOT. HE WILL MAKE AMERICA GREAT AGAIN, KEEP AMERICA GREAT AND SAVE AMERICA. AND I HAPPEN TO LOVE HIM AND OUR USA.

TO ALL FOREIGN ADVERSARIES OF OUR GREAT UNITED STATES OF AMERICA—IF YOU PLAN TO HARM / TRY TO HARM / HARM PRESIDENT DONALD J. TRUMP WE WILL HIT YOU BACK 10 TO 15 TIMES HARDER.

IF I WIN THE PRESIDENTIAL ELECTION IN NOV 2028, I WILL BE TRUE TO THIS AS THE 48TH PRESIDENT OF THE UNITED STATES OF AMERICA.

THIS IS A CAMPAIGN PROMISE.

GARY BARVE

DATING LIFE: MY PROMISE

I have been thinking about whether I should make this post on campaign social media, and I have decided to make the post:

In the previous few years, I have made multiple posts on campaign social media about my dating life and my dating preference.

First, and very importantly I want to say this to our American people:

I love our African American or Black American people, I love our Brown American people (I'm Brown!) and I love our Caucasian American or White American people: I Love People Who Love The United States of America and Who Support President Trump!

However when it comes to my dating life and my dating preference, I have realized that I am romantically attracted to only Caucasian or White women. As I have said before, the chemistry I share and the vibe I share on a date with a Caucasian or White woman is incredible. Now, obviously not all dates result in a friendship or a romantic relationship, but the time shared with the Caucasian or White woman on the date is on many or most occasions really awesome and great.

Also, while I tremendously respect, like and admire many women who are not Caucasian or White, and I have female friends who are not Caucasian or White, I just do not feel romantically attracted to them. That is just how I am, and I do not feel I should be in any way trying to hide this fact from our great American people.

Here is what I also believe: The 2028 Presidential election is going to be a tough battle, the Republican Primary Election as well as the General Election if I am the Republican Nominee.

It is my strong belief and opinion that my political opponents will try and make it very difficult for me to date a woman who is Caucasian or White by various political tactics such as for example, calling me a White Supremacist or a racist.

I know for a fact that I am none of these things. Along with many friends who are Caucasian or White, I also have many friends who are African American and who are Brown American, and I really love and enjoy their company and friendship.

So, to mitigate any political attacks against me on the topic of my dating life, I am making a promise that I will only have as my girlfriend and also my future wife a woman who is White or Caucasian. And as you know, I have a reputation in the political realm that I always keep (and I always will keep) all my promises.

I feel having this promise will be correct for me, and also for my Presidential campaign, because I will be able to campaign with a positive mindset.

And now I will say this to ALL our American people:

Vote for me not because of my dating preference, but because I am a great American patriot ready to take a bullet for my country and I am ready to go to jail for my country because of the political weaponization of the DOJ by the corrupt democrat party.

Vote for me because I will fix our Southern Border and courageously and fearlessly fight against criminal gangs and cartels such as TREN de ARAGUA and MS 13 to keep our American people safe and secure.

Vote for me because I am the biggest supporter of our Police, Sheriffs, ICE, Military, Veterans, Fire Fighters and First Responders.

Vote for me because I am a loyal supporter of our President Donald J. Trump for many years, and I have proven myself to be the biggest supporter of President Donald J. Trump in the country.

And vote for me because I love our United States of America, I love President Donald J. Trump and I love our great American people, and because I will fight for YOU our American people irrespective of your race and I will help Make America Great Again, Keep America Great and Save America.

Gary Barve

On Nov 15, 2022 President Donald J. Trump announced he is running for President of The United States of America in the 2024 election.

Gary Barve: While I respect all religions, I am Christian. I believe Jesus Christ is with President Trump and he will win the election.

Indictment 1, Indictment 2, Indictment 3, Indictment 4 against President Trump because of the political weaponization of the DOJ by the corrupt democrat party.

Gary Barve: While I respect all religions, I am Christian. I believe Jesus Christ is with President Trump and he will win the election.

Assassination Attempt 1, Assassination Attempt 2 against President Trump.

Gary Barve: While I respect all religions, I am Christian. I believe Jesus Christ is with President Trump and he will win the election.

President Donald J. Trump wins the election and becomes the 47th President of The United States of America.

Gary Barve: I believe in you President Trump more than just about anyone else in the country. You are an inspiration for me, and I love you for the positive impact you have had on my life and because you fight for our country with infinite love and faith for our American people. I would appreciate the opportunity to meet with you again and learn from your wisdom and advice. Thank you for the work you have done for our country, for the work you are doing for our country, and for the work you will do for our country to Make America Great Again, Keep America Great and Save America.

I am including the link to the video of my speech given by me on July 13, 2024 few moments after the horrific assasination attempt to show my love, support, solidarity with President Trump and to express my unshakable belief that Jesus Christ is with President Trump, Jesus Christ is with our country and Jesus Christ is with our great American people and that President Trump will win the election and become the 47th President of The USA.

In Christ,

Gary Barve

MY DIRECT MESSAGE TO ALL PERSONNEL TRYING TO DESTROY ME POLITICALLY:

In the previous few days and weeks, I have met many people. Most have been polite and nice to me, and have been supportive of my campaign for President of The USA in the 2028 election as a Republican supporter of President Donald J. Trump.

A select few people however, I believe have tried to or are trying to destroy me politically.

My direct message to these select few people is this—Try and destroy me politically at your own risk. Like President Donald J. Trump, I believe in an Eye for an Eye, and per his advice in his books and interviews, I will fight back 10 to 15 times stronger in the political arena at the right time.

I am in the 2028 Presidential election to WIN as a Republican supporter of President Donald J. Trump, so that I can serve our great American people and help Make America Great Again, Keep America Great and Save America as the 48th President of The USA.

Gary Barve

◇◇◇

Dear Americans,

I will be filing my initial paperwork very soon and officially become a candidate for President of The United States of America in the 2028 election as a Republican supporter of President Donald J. Trump.

During the course of the next approximately 4 years, I believe there are a few things about me that will be used against me by my opponents.

I am 100% committed to my campaign for President of The United States of America in the 2028 election as a supporter of President Donald J. Trump and I am choosing to mention these things about me here:

ONE:

As you know, I was diagnosed with clinical depression related illness in approximately year 2012. I believe the symptoms for my clinical depression related illness had started showing in year 2009 itself. (I have now made a complete recovery and take no treatment).

In I think year 2011, I was in Europe and I paid for sex in two countries: Slovakia and Germany. I think I was about 26 years old at that time and I remember I cried and was depressed on most of this visit to Europe.

In approximately December 2017 I was admitted to the hospital for what was my worst episode of clinical depression related illness. After being discharged from the hospital, I took a trip to Costa Rica in approximately January 2018 and paid for sex there.

I HAVE OBTAINED LEGAL CLARIFICATION THAT I HAVE NOT VIOLATED ANY LAWS.

I am not proud of these decisions I made many years back under termendous depression duress. I will never get invloved in such actions and decisions again in my life.

I apologize to Jesus Christ as my Lord and Savior, to my parents and to my friends for having made such decisions many years back under termendous depression duress.

I am a believer in Jesus Christ as my Lord and Savior, and few years back I got baptized. Becoming a believer in Jesus Christ as my Lord and Savior has given me tremendous purpose in my life. So has my drive and goal of serving our great American people.

I believe what I shared with you in this point ONE is an issue personal to me and I will not elaborate on this issue or talk about it in the media.

TWO:

I am sharing a detail here which to be honest is not easy for me to share with you, because I am going to be ridiculed by some of my opponents, some in the media and some democrat constituents: From grade 5 to grade 12 (I was born in the USA but did most of my school in India) in India, I was bullied immensely by many of my peers including by some of my teachers. This included verbal bullying and some physical bullying. Some of my peers were nice to me and I did have friends, and some of my teachers were nice to me too, but some were not.

I feel one of the reasons for this is I changed schools at grade 5, and to be honest I have recently realized that this school was not exactly the greatest. I believe I reacted to this immense bullying by crossdressing in the privacy of my parents house in India, and never in front of other people. To my memory, the last time I did this was year 2003, and I have not done this in the previous approximately 21 years, and never will. I believe there are some people other than me who know about this, and I am sharing these details with you.

I believe bullying in schools is really horrible and should not happen—verbal or physical. I also want to say that I am against the concept of transgender, and believe this should never be taught to children.

I believe what I shared with you in this point TWO is an issue personal to me and I will not elaborate on this issue or talk about it in the media.

THREE:

As you know, for many years I suffered from clinical depression related illness. I am happy to say that I have made a complete recovery and take no treatment now and I thank my Lord and Savior Jesus Christ, my parents, my friends and the medical personnel for giving me the courage and ability to conquer this illness.

To my memory, in approximately year 2014 I was suffering from a massive anxiety episode at my parents home in Santa Clara, CA where I was living at that time. During my anxiety episode, I went ahead and created an online account on a website that to my memory was meant for dating for people with STD's. I had previously had a rash on my torso and I showed it to a doctor who to my memory said it could perhaps be an STD called HPV. The rash went away and never has returned, and my personal belief is I never had HPV. In my anxiety episode I created the mentioned online account.

VERY IMPORTANTLY I WANT TO CLARIFY THAT I HAVE TAKEN MULTIPLE STD TESTS INCLUDING A STD TEST QUITE RECENTLY AND ALL STD TESTS HAVE ALWAYS HAD 100% CLEAN RESULTS.

I believe what I shared with you in this point THREE is an issue personal to me and I will not elaborate on this issue or talk about it in the media.

FOUR:

I made a post on campaign social media on January 19, 2024 about my dating life. I support this campaign social media post. I like to date caucasian or white women and would definitely like to have as my girlfriend and someday my wife a caucasian or white woman.

In the previous few years, I have been on many dates with caucasian or white women, and while not all dates have worked out into a romantic relationship or a strong friendship, I feel the chemistry and vibe I shared with many of the caucasian or white women I had the great pleasure of going out on a date with was awesome!

The change between my campaign social media post on January 19, 2024 and today is that I am now again open to dating and I am open to not staying single anymore.

I will also say this—I love our African American people or Black American people, I love our Brown American people, I love our Caucasian American or White American people: I love people who love our USA and support President Trump. Vote for me not because of my dating preference, but vote for me because I love President Trump, I love our United States of America, and I love our great American people and I will fight for YOU the American people irrespective of your race and I will help President Trump Make America Great Again!

FIVE:

I am now residing in West Des Moines, Iowa and I am enjoying living here. Iowa is the first in the nation caucus election, the people in Iowa are very friendly and incredible and there are many great American farmers in Iowa.

My friends, as I reflect upon some of the tough situations I have been through in my life, I find it really incredible that I have managed to run for City Council in Santa Clara, CA in the 2020 election as a supporter of President Trump, for US Congress in Florida in the 2024 Primary election as a supporter of President Trump, and will soon officially be a candidate for President of The United States of America in the 2028 election as a supporter of President Trump.

While I am very happy about this acheivement, I also give tremendous thanks for this acheivement to my belief in Jesus Christ as my Lord and Savior, to President Donald J. Trump's inspirational books such as Think Big and his patriotic courageous leadership, to my parents for their support, to my friends, to my country the greatest country in the world The United States of America and to YOU our great American people for showing the faith and confidence in me.

I FEEL IT IS NOT ALWAYS ABOUT THE CHALLENGES AND OBSTACLES THAT YOU FACE IN LIFE, BUT IT IS ABOUT HOW YOU FIGHT BACK FROM THE CHALLENGES AND OBSTACLES THAT YOU FACE IN LIFE.

Announcement about my official candidacy for President of The United States of America in the 2028 election as a Republican supporter of President Donald J. Trump will be made soon. I have begun forming a team, and will soon have personnel joining the campaign in Iowa, Florida and Virginia.

Lets Make America Great Again, Keep America Great and Save America as huge supporters of President Donald J. Trump!

In Christ,

Gary Barve

◇◇◇

Congratulations to the 47th President of The United States of America, President Donald J. Trump for a great WIN!

Gary Barve

ILLEGAL IMMIGRANTS IN OUR USA SHOULD BE DEPORTED BACK TO THEIR COUNTRY OF ORIGIN AND OUR AMERICAN PEOPLE SHOULD NOT BEAR THE FINANCIAL BURDEN FOR THE DEPORTATIONS WHEREVER PRACTICALLY POSSIBLE

I had said in an interview few days prior to Nov 5, 2024 that when President Trump wins the Presidency, we will kick out of our country or incarcerate members of illegal criminal gangs such as TREN de ARAGUA and MS 13.

I was not joking.

Gang members should wisely leave our country immediately! GET OUT NOW. AND NEVER COME BACK TO THE USA.

Also, all people in our country illegally—and there are probably about 20 Million of them—should be deported back to their country of origin. I support LEGAL LAWFUL IMMIGRATION. I do not support ILLEGAL IMMIGRATION.

I believe our great American Police, Sheriffs, ICE and if required our Military and even our Veterans should be given complete freedom and authority within the bounds of law and order to do their jobs and complete the deportations of illegal immigrants.

Also, why should the American people bear financial burden for these deportations? It is not the American people's fault, and wherever practical the American people should not pay for the deportations via their hard earned tax dollars.

The country of origin from where the illegal immigrant came to our USA should bear the cost of the deportation. Not you, our great American people!

I will be sharing my thoughts about this policy with personnel from President Trump's team when possible.

I have already made a campaign promise that I will support President Trump's America First agenda 100% until Nov 2028, and that after Nov 2028 if I am elected President of The USA I will make decisions for our USA keeping America First and our American People First. I will keep this (and all) my promises.

AMERICA IS TRUMP COUNTRY.

Gary Barve

UNSUNG HEROES: POLICE, SHERIFFS, ICE, MILITARY, VETERANS, FIRE FIGHTERS, FIRST RESPONDERS

As a candidate running for President of The United States of America as a Republican supporter of President Donald J. Trump, and as a former City Council and US Congress candidate as a President Trump supporter, I have received some recognition via a little bit of Press Coverage and Media Attention, and have been able to courageously talk about my positions against crime, gangs such as TREN de ARAGUA, MS-13 and illegal immigration.

However I genuinely believe that our POLICE, SHERIFFS, ICE, MILITARY, VETERANS, FIRE FIGHTERS, FIRST RESPONDERS are our UNSUNG HEROES. They do not always get the recognition they deserve, and are more courageous than most people running for elected office including me. At the same time, I feel they are poorly compensated from a salary perspective in many jurisdictions in our country.

There are many other professions that start with huge salaries, and their job descriptions do not require them to risk their lives for our American people on a daily basis. While I have nothing against huge salaries for these other professions, I believe our POLICE, SHERIFFS, ICE, MILITARY, VETERANS, FIRE FIGHTERS, FIRST RESPONDERS should be better compensated.

I have already made a campaign promise that I will support President Trump's America First agenda 100% until Nov 2028, and that after Nov 2028 if I am elected President of The USA I will make decisions for our USA keeping America First and our American People First.

I will keep this (and all) my promises, and in line with my promises I will push for and promote the idea of better and just compensation for our UNSUNG HEROES if I am elected 48th President of The USA in Nov 2028, and will happily talk about it during my Presidential campaign.

This is my campaign promise to you our great American people.

AMERICA IS TRUMP COUNTRY.

Gary Barve

◇◇◇

I love Israel and I am a BIG supporter of Israel. I believe Israel is our friend and ally.

However, I will say this and I will say this very happily and proudly: There is one country in the world that I love infinitely more than any other country in the world. That country is our great country THE UNITED STATES OF AMERICA.

Gary Barve

◇◇◇

America has spent over $100 BILLION on Ukraine in the Russia–Ukraine conflict. For a fraction of this amount, America can GET EVERY HOMELESS GREAT AMERICAN VETERAN OFF THE STREETS!

I want ZERO VETERAN HOMELESSNESS, ZERO VETERAN JOBLESSNESS AND COMPLETE MENTAL HEALTH SERVICES FOR OUR GREAT AMERICAN VETERANS.

I have made a campaign promise that I will support President Trump's America First agenda 100% until Nov 2028, and if I am elected President of The USA in Nov 2028 I will make decisions for our country keeping America First and our American People First. I will keep all my promises.

I am going to talk about this initiative with personnel who worked with President Trump's campaign.

I will support this initiative if I get elected the 48th President of The USA. This is a Campaign Promise.

Our great American Veterans put their lives on the line to serve YOU. Now WE SERVE AND SUPPORT OUR GREAT AMERICAN VETERANS.

Gary Barve

I had the great opportunity to attend the Minnesota Young Republicans Christmas Party event in Minnesota on December 10, 2024. I met with and had conversations with just about every person attending the event, and shared details about my campaign for President of The United States of America in the 2028 election as a Republican supporter of President Donald J. Trump.

I say this to our great American young people: You have the greatest personality, the greatest intellect and the greatest passion and enthusiasm for living life. You are meant to achieve great things for yourself and for America. Never Give Up and Keep Moving Forward, you will be successful.

I believe our great American patriotic young people have tremendous potential, and with the right leadership our country will continue to be the greatest country in the world for the future.

Similarly, our great American patriotic seniors have the courage, experience and love for our country to be able to successfully help President Donald J. Trump Make America Great Again and to also guide our young people, including me, to success, and help Keep America Great for the future.

My campaign for President of The United States of America as a Republican supporter of President Donald

J. Trump will see great support from our great American patriotic youth and great American patriotic seniors.

Make America Great Again, Keep America Great and Save America.

Gary Barve

Going forward on many occasions I will be referring to the democrat party as THE KAMALA DEMOCRAT PARTY.

KAMALA was the democrat nominee in the previous 2024 Presidential election cycle and is effectively holding the flag of the democrat party. Kamala led her KAMALA DEMOCRAT PARTY to a historic DEFEAT losing all 7 battleground states one after the next.

PRESIDENT DONALD J. TRUMP led his Republican Party and our great USA to a landslide victory against all odds in the GREATEST POLITICAL COMEBACK in the history of our USA.

I will say this—THERE ARE MANY DEMOCRAT PARTY CONSTITUENTS, THAT IS THE DEMOCRAT PARTY VOTERS WHO ARE GREAT PEOPLE WHO LOVE OUR USA BUT ARE MISGUIDED BY FAKE NEWS MEDIA SUCH AS CNN AND MSNBC.

I WELCOME ALL DEMOCRAT AND INDEPENDENT CONSTITUENTS AND VOTERS WHO TRULY LOVE OUR USA TO JOIN PRESIDENT DONALD J. TRUMP'S AMERICA FIRST REPUBLICAN PARTY AND BE A PART OF THE MOVEMENT THAT WILL MAKE AMERICA GREAT AGAIN, KEEP AMERICA GREAT AND SAVE AMERICA.

Gary Barve

◇◇

Yesterday on Nov 16, 2024 I had the honor of attending The Trump Force 47 event in Michigan.

I met some awesome patriotic American people who volunteered for President Donald J. Trump's campaign for President of The USA.

I appreciate the work our patriotic American volunteers performed for President Donald J. Trump's Presidential campaign, they took valuable time from their busy lives and work days to serve our country by volunteering for President Donald J. Trump's Presidential campaign and helping him achieve a massive WIN for our USA on Nov 5, 2024.

America Is Trump Country!

Gary Barve

◇◇

Tomorrow Nov 5, 2024 is the most important election in the history of our great United States of America.

I humbly ask you to please VOTE FOR PRESIDENT DONALD J. TRUMP.

I am confident that he will WIN and be the 47th President of The United States of America.

Gary Barve

〈◇◇◇〉

MY NAME IS GARY BARVE. I AM RUNNING FOR PRESIDENT OF THE UNITED STATES OF AMERICA IN THE 2028 ELECTION BECAUSE I LOVE PRESIDENT DONALD J. TRUMP, I LOVE OUR GREAT UNITED STATES OF AMERICA AND I LOVE OUR GREAT AMERICAN PEOPLE, AND I WANT TO HELP PRESIDENT DONALD J. TRUMP MAKE AMERICA GREAT AGAIN, KEEP AMERICA GREAT AND SAVE AMERICA.

AMERICA RUNS THROUGH MY BLOOD BODY MIND AND SOUL.

GARY BARVE

Gary Barve's Social Media is:

Campaign Website: www.GaryBarveForAmerica.com

Campaign Truth Social Page:
https://truthsocial.com/@GaryBarve

Campaign Facebook Page:
https://www.facebook.com/GaryBarveForUSA

Campaign X.com Page:
https://x.com/garybarveusa?s=21